30 YEARS WITH COMPUTERS

(and other narrow opinions)

John T. Benton

Have fun at work!
John

Published by: Executive Information Development
Company, Publishing Division,
121 South Drive, Tower Lakes Estates,
Barrington, Illinois 60010-1324

John T. Benton
March 1997

Benton, John T.
30 Years with Computers

Illustrations and Cover: Jay Ohlrich

Printed in the United States of America

Library of Congress Catalog Number: 91-72528

ISBN: 0-9629271-0-4

ACKNOWLEDGMENTS

Appreciation is expressed to the following individuals for their experience sharing, knowledge and tolerance for the author:

R. J. Flynn, a long time friend who said, "We should write a book." This is the first, maybe he will do the second. Bob is a fellow comrade in the battle for quality and productivity in the face of corporate dysfunction.

E. Patrick Lira, another long time business associate. Pat has great insight, enthusiasm and humor. He has always been supportive and challenging in his direction of productive activities.

Harold Keech, a high school principal who knew what a high school was supposed to provide and delivered quality products, kids with someplace to go.

Shelby Carter, one of the few excellent managers I have had the privilege of being associated with. I am really thankful for his insight and guidance early in my career.

My weekly breakfast buddy, Glen Bretsnyder, who keeps me informed and up to date on the latest microcomputer announcements.

Robert Martin, whose energetic, dynamic and risk taking activities are a great lesson in getting things done. He is truly an entrepreneur with a vision.

The many productive and talented people, too numerous to mention, who I have been associated with, that have somehow stayed afloat in the raging sea of mediocre, self-serving individuals in the business world.

INTRODUCTION

This book consists of fictionalized versions of real events and general commentary on the varied environments found in the information processing industry. (Names have been changed to protect both the innocent and the guilty.) It is based on my work with electronic components and computers since 1958. I believe that some of the experiences might be useful to others.

The culture changes encountered within the computing industry are implicit in the book and, of course, will be more readily recognized by those that have worked in this industry. If you have worked in the computer industry, you will recognize many of the personality types.

I consider myself fortunate and am thankful for the many experiences I have had in the computer industry. The mutually beneficial relationships with IBM, The Service Bureau Corporation/Control Data Corporation, as well as my own independent consulting clients have contributed to the content in this book.

My formal education background, involvement in aerospace, medicine, agricultural research, systems engineering and commercial data processing have also provided the background from which my experience grew.

This book does not have a "front to back" design, and you may wish to read the chapters randomly. Although many are topically related, most chapters can stand alone as individual essays.

FOREWORD

My favorite story is "The Brochure." It illustrates so clearly how corporate managers can lose perspective in what they are trying to accomplish for reasons that have nothing to do with the job to be done. The story also gives the reader a good insight into the great story-telling ability of the author. He is well-read and has a phenomenal memory for the right quote, the right poem, or, in most cases, the right humorous anecdote.

The author enjoys the sport of people watching, and individual corporate managers have provided him with many amusing stories and enough material for many books. In our discussions, he has often commented on how easily a manager can allow his ego to lead him astray. None of us is free from this malady; but certain individuals seem to contract this disease of egotism to such a degree that they are severely crippled in their decision making capability.

Problem solving is difficult enough without putting on blinders and placing roadblocks in the way. The author is an excellent problem-solver, not only because he is a professional in his field, but also because, as he puts it, he *"leaves his ego at the door"* when he enters a business meeting. The twinkle in his eye not only shows his enjoyment for life, but also his wisdom and understanding of our human foibles.

John has artfully provided us, in a very humorous way, an excellent guide to his specialty of people watching. What should bother every corporate manager who reads this book is that the stories are valid! Remember, there may be others who are reading this book—and they are watching *you!*

Robert J. Flynn

Table of Contents

H.Q.

I. HEADQUARTERS

The most important goal of any organization is the growth and development of the individuals within that organization and their contribution to the society in which they live.

CHAPTER 1

THE NEW TITLE

The New Opportunities

In the late 1960s, the computer industry was beginning to change to a consumer-based environment. The advent of time-sharing based processing with ready-made applications, allowed individualized functional and departmental computing to exist without having to deal with the fixed schedule and long development cycle of data processing departments. This, of course, preceded the explosive use of minicomputers and time-sharing systems beginning in the late 1960s and early 1970s.

Many companies or divisions of companies evolved in this new industry. As a result, many new professional positions were created. Many service providers rushed to this marketplace. There was also a proliferation of many local applications, geographically dispersed, put on central time-sharing systems without adequate support. There was a real need to coordinate these applications, support the non-data processing end users, and expand the marketplace.

Results of a Manager's Meeting

A new position had to be created to manage the marketing and broad use of computer applications in an arena of non-computer literate customers which varied widely in both capability and geography. It was decided that a job description be developed for the new position of Director of Applications Development. Richie Greenman was awarded this position and soon discovered that the description was a list of all the things that the VP of Marketing did not like to do. Furthermore, this VP gave Richie the people he did not want on his own staff. Richie started out with about ten people. Three were managers. Two of the managers were a little "weak," resulting in some correspondence that illustrated his frustration.

The First Letter

From: Director of Applications Development

February 16, 19xx

To: Staff

Subject: Vacation

I will be on vacation during the week of February 21 through February 25. In my absence, Clyde Streetman will be responsible for the Applications Development Department. In my absence, all personnel are encouraged to solve their own problems.

R. T. Greenman

A Few Months Later

From: Director of Applications Development

July 1, 19xx

To: Staff

Subject: Vacation

I will be on vacation from Friday, July 2, until Monday, July 12. In my absence, Clyde Streetman will be responsible for the Applications Development Department. In my absence, all personnel are encouraged to solve their own problems.

R. T. Greenman

Christmas

From: Director of Applications Development

December 8, 19xx

To: All Staff

Subject: Christmas

Christmas is a religious holiday. In the U. S. A., we have made it a retail bonanza. I regret this.

People should at least be given the privacy to celebrate Christmas the way they want to celebrate Christmas, not the way they may be forced to celebrate it. Therefore, I would like to make the following suggestion:

In our offices we will not celebrate it in any formal manner. There will be no compulsory exchange of cards, gifts or grabbing at each other under the mistletoe.

On the other hand, if any individual wishes to do any of the above things or many that I haven't mentioned, go right ahead. Believe me, nobody likes Christmas any more than I do, and I wish you all a truly joyful holiday season.

R. T. Greenman

The Move

TO: Clyde, Croddy, Rollie, John B. Terry, Tom, Lou, Ray, John R., Chris, George, Stephen, Ted, Bianca, Jim, Barry, Dave, Paul, Merle, Tony, and Anna.

CC: Steve, Nancy, Tommy, Gus, Bud

From: R. T. Greenman, Director of Applications Development

Subject: NOLITE MOVERE AD NEW HQ!

(Loosely translated, this means we ain't gonna move as scheduled.)

In order to ensure greater tranquility for the common man, to provide for completed facilities for all inhabitants and preclude a week of computer outage, we have cancelled the anticipated move date of Thursday, March 7. Hopefully, we will move on Thursday March 14, the eve of the Ides of March and me mither's 85th birthday, availability of elevators permitting.

That's the bad news. The good news is that you can distribute your packing over another seven days and make a real go for the Cherry Ripple Champagne packer's prize.

Given the packing that has already been done, it's no fair to ask Anna to find the January, 1971 issue of Confuserworld.

We'll alert you ASAP regarding a firm move date. Thanks for

your patience in our temporarily suspended Chinese fire drill.

Richie

Fortunately, Richie had a sense of humor. He was a hard driving individual. He had excellent sales and management skills. Technically, he was weak, but he knew how to determine when someone was conning him. He depended on the people that worked for him. He did have to be reminded to say thanks once in a while.

CHAPTER 2

THE BROCHURE

I spent a *short* time near the top of a corporate hierarchy which included some memorable experiences of getting things done. There were also unusual involvements with some interesting people, both in terms of their personalities and their capabilities. This is a part of the scenario occurring just before the release of a very profitable software application.

The software was developed by a third party vendor—very talented, very wealthy, and with a higher ego level than most people's. His name is R. T. Highman, but he was known as "Robbie." I referred to him as "Rapid Robbie."

The Director of Applications Development was a true blue, gung ho company man. He had been a top salesman, was a good manager, and an Ivy League school graduate. He wore expensive suits of the three piece variety with a starched white shirt, rep ties with the coordinated pocket handkerchief, wingtip shoes, and those thin black socks that you pull up to your armpits. He was very talented, reasonably wealthy, and also had a higher ego level than most people's. His name is

R. T. Greenman, another obviously fictitious name chosen to protect the guilty. He will hereafter be referred to as "Richie." Richie was the newly appointed Director of Applications Development mentioned in the previous and subsequent chapters.

I was the project administrator and had to satisfy both of these individuals. Both were pleasant and reasonable enough to deal with as long as the conversation did not include mention of the other person.

Rollie McFarsky, another more mature and experienced project administrator, and a good friend, was the person responsible for my promotion into this corporate maze. Rollie was a cool Irishman (now there's an oxymoron) who I often conferred with when confronted with a knotty problem. I tried to make him feel guilty for getting me into this situation. He has a really nasty laugh.

Rollie and I, along with our communications, advertising and publications personnel, had designed a good three color brochure with gray scale pictures. It had been approved by Robbie and he was anxious to see it hit the marketplace. We took it to Richie with all the approvals and recommendations. Richie said it looked great, but we would have to hold off on it because we had budget problems. He suggested that we do a flyer type brochure in the interim until our revenues were up.

I patiently spent some time pointing out that we already had six months of development behind us and that the product timing with our sales kickoffs was right. Now was the time for us to regain the confidence of the sales force with a quality product, quality presentation and promotional materials. The cost of the brochure was very small compared to the rest of the expenses and development costs. I chose not to mention the damage it would do to our vendor relationship.

Richie persisted, saying that his hands were tied and he had no choice. I was about to accuse him of a childish personal vendetta against Robbie, when Rollie, who could see my color changing, intervened. He told Richie that we would call our publications department to see what we could do.

Rollie and I went to his office and closed the door. We were both silent for a long time. I finally made a bitter comment, recalling Imhoff's Law, which states: *"The organization of any bureaucracy is very much like a septic tank—the really big chunks rise to the top."*

We called our publications guy, Tyler, and explained the situation to him. Tyler was another member of our underground cadre. He could get things done! Rollie asked him what kind of paper stock he had. Tyler gave us a rundown on volumes and costs of what he had on hand.

> *"At last, in desperation, we tried a trick called inversion, described in Edward deBono's* Lateral Thinking. *When you're stuck trying to solve a problem, deBono suggests that rather than looking for ways to achieve your goal, look for ways to achieve the exact opposite of your goal."*
>
> DeMarco and Lister

Rollie, Tyler and I executed the approach of *"quality reduction of the product"* as described by DeMarco and Lister.

We re-oriented the eight page brochure to a four page flyer with the pictures and some of the text taken out. We used the worst quality (lowest cost, right?), diarrhea brown stock we could find, did a preliminary printing for the Branch Manager's

Meeting two weeks hence. Black print on brown, and I do mean *brown* stock, as a sales piece? We told Tyler to keep it under wraps. The flyers were not to be seen until they were opened at the Branch Manager's meeting.

We showed Richie the four page layout, but not the color. We told him we were doing it as inexpensively as possible, which was the truth. He approved it for publication. We were surprised that he didn't ask us more detailed questions. He was probably preoccupied and feeling satisfied that he was sticking it to Robbie, and he wore a "Cheshire Cat" grin. (Apparently he had not recalled the whole story of "Alice in Wonderland.")

The day of the Branch Managers meeting arrived. I took some vacation days. I don't remember what Rollie did. He did make some remarks to me about cowardice, but I preferred to call it discretion.

I don't know exactly what happened, but there were rumors and threats of mob action and ranting and raving at the meeting. The Vice-President of Marketing thought it was pretty funny. Richie was fairly upset for a while. I heard that Richie tried to call Rollie, Tyler, and me, but we were all "someplace else." The Budget was rapidly approved for the original brochure and it was in the Sales offices within two weeks. Tyler had already scheduled the printer before the Branch Manager's meeting even took place. Tyler commented: *"All progress is the result of crisis."*

Taking the advice of "Direct Dan," the Divisional Vice President, Richie cooled off. The VP convinced Richie that he should appreciate the fact that he had creative problem solvers working for him. Richie took some well deserved heat from the field, but he did not seek vengeance, at least not immediately. Overall, he was a good manager.

After this experience, Richie was always more thorough and reasonable with Rollie and me .

By the way, this product turned the revenues around markedly and Richie was promoted to VP of Marketing *and* Applications Development.

CHAPTER 3

CONTRACT RENEGOTIATION

The new product was now generating significant revenues. The vendor, Robbie, believed that he was "being had," and he was not completely wrong in his assertions. By now, the application development staff had grown. I was in charge of administering, investigating and implementing several projects. Two inside developers of another one of our high revenue applications were promoted to administrative positions to manage the project managers. Their expertise as managers, however, was not adequate. They went "by the book," and in general were fearful of anything that was not in the procedure manual.

My manager, Croddy, had tried to talk with Robbie several times. He tried to get Richie Greenman, now the VP of Marketing and Applications Development, and Robbie together to iron out their differences. I strongly advised against this plan. It was like putting dynamite and nitro-glycerin in the same room.

At this point, I had worked with Robbie for over a year. I'd had arguments with him, but I had always been honest with him and he respected me. We already had too many people talking with him and the issues of further development and expansion of his very successful product were headed "down the crapper."

Croddy, Rollie and I sat down with the lawyer, Bob Maples. Bob was not your typical lawyer. He had been with the corporation for a long time and was a savvy businessman. I asked Bob to come up with an agreement that would be as fair as possible and easy to administer with our somewhat antiquated accounting facility on the computer system. The object was to get all of the internal approvals necessary and go with an all or nothing scenario. Croddy offered to take it to Richie, who had recently been promoted to VP of Marketing and Applications Development. I suggested Bob take it to Richie and the Divisional VP, one on one. A corporate lawyer has a little more power than someone in a weak staff management position. I suggested that I be put back on the project as the only contact for Robbie, the vendor. *Reluctantly,* this was approved. Progress requires a limited bureaucracy, and the present rampant bureaucracy was destined for failure.

> *"The organization is armed only with precedents, a trained incapacity—vested thoughtways that lead them directly to ruin.... New situations demand precisely the kind of skills that traditional bureaucracies crush."*
>
> William L. Livingston

I picked up the phone. When Robbie found that he had only me to deal with, his reaction was favorable. He was nearly in tears from frustration in his dealings with us. I told him that we were working with the Corporate Lawyers to come up with as fair a deal as we could, but that it probably would not satisfy all his desires. He was somewhat recalcitrant and told me not to bother. He would take his updated projects elsewhere. Then we had the following exchange:

"Robbie, do you really want to go through with another vendor what you went through with us?"

"The other vendors agree that you are giving me a raw deal?"

"No crap! What else would competition say?"

"Well, I am talking with them anyway."

"And in the meantime, your product is being stalled here, not growing, and they are investigating other resources to be competitive with you if you don't tumble in bed with them."

"I hadn't really thought about that."

"I would like to fly down to meet you when I get the agreement. Would you at least look at it?"

"Is this going to be another meeting with Richie or Croddy?"

"No."

After a long pause, Robbie said, "OK. Who else will be sitting in on the negotiation?"

"Robbie, there is no more negotiation. I am coming down alone with the agreement. I am going to help you make a career decision. If you sign it, we move ahead. If not, you can pursue your plans with competitors. We will freeze the present product and contract. We will then pursue our own applications development. In the interest of everybody's sanity, this has to be resolved. When we tie up two or three corporate attorneys, a Company President, a couple of VPs, Directors and a peon like me, we will resolve issues. Please don't interpret this as a threat. It is in everybody's best interest, including yours."

"John, you are not a peon. OK, it can't hurt to look."

The agreement was finally drawn up. My immediate manager, Croddy, asked when we were going to fly down to Richmond. I told Croddy that he was not going. Needless to say, there were a couple of days worth of management run around before that issue was resolved. Surprisingly, Richie told Croddy that I should handle this situation alone. I also insisted that the contract be signed by our people before I left for Richmond. This, of course, was very unorthodox, but I also won that battle, thanks to Bob Maples. Bob told me I owed him one steak dinner already, and another one if Robbie signed. I never could figure out lawyers.

> *" ... but managers are not usually part of the teams that they manage. Teams are made up of peers, equals that function as equals."*
>
> DeMarco and Lister

I called Robbie and made an appointment. I rented a car and drove to his very nice, luxurious home where he also had his office. I arrived at about 9:00 AM. I had open reservations for the flight back to New York.

We talked at length about the present status of the product. We spent a lot of time talking about the fact that a corporation provides the structure and empowerment for the actual functions that make money for an organization. I also pointed out that bureaucracy and personality conflicts are a part of this and really have to be put in perspective. Robbie showed me some of the applications he had developed and others he was investigating. He was a very valuable resource person that the company should keep, but, he also had to be dealt with both fairly and firmly.

The time is about 2:00 PM.

Robbie sighed and said, "This is fun, but I suppose we should look at the agreement?"

The phone rang. It was Croddy asking me how things were going. My first reaction was to jump down his throat, but Robbie was sitting right there. Instead, I took the opportunity to talk about all the development that was complete and what Robbie was doing. I also told Croddy that it looked like we had a great future if Robbie had more cooperation from us than in the past. In other words, I kept talking about how wonderful the product was until Croddy said he had another call. I think he was getting nauseated.

"Thanks, John. That was very kind."

"It's only the truth Robbie."

"Do you want a drink?"

"After you sign the agreement." (We both laughed.)

I gave the agreement to Robbie and started working on things I took out of my briefcase. He studied the paper for about thirty minutes and then put the agreement on the table. There was a long silence. The clock gonged. It was 3:00 PM.

"The issue of data base usage is still unresolved."

"Robbie, you are correct on the data base issue. I argued long and hard. Here is a letter I wrote to the development lab several weeks ago addressing that issue. I included your suggestions."

"Why don't they listen?"

"Robbie, this is one of those issues you are going to have to swallow. The system accounting programs don't handle transaction counting at this point and we are expanding our application base rather than resolving your singular problem. We believe that this is an appropriate priority and valid business decision. This contract is as good as you are going to get and I for one will respect you and your decision either way."

We discussed this and many similar issues with many intervening silences. The clock gonged. It was 5:00 PM.

"What about your plane?"

"Do you want me to walk out of here with an unsigned contract?"

After another long pause, Robbie said, "Do you want a drink?"

"OK, then I want to tell you a story."

Robbie got us a couple of Scotches and some cheese and crackers. We made some small talk about family, the general business climate, etc. Then I returned to the issues at hand.

"In any contract, between two parties, there is seldom complete satisfaction. Each party has to give up something. Each party must benefit. I think that this is what you see in front of you. Look at the benefits from your point of view. If it is any help to you, Richie fought this, and I used a Corporate Lawyer to beat him up. This is an agreement from the Corporation, not an ego driven individual. If you don't sign it, you'll hurt us both. You have to put some of your ego injury behind you, too. We really don't want to hurt each other, do we?"

"No. What was the story you were going to tell me?"

(Another Scotch, too.)

(Author's Note: Apologies to those who may object to the sexist nature of the following.)

"There was this beautiful, young blonde of outstanding proportions that had a toothache. She made an appointment with the dentist. Upon her arrival at the dentist's office, she found herself in the dental chair with a very young dentist looking into her mouth. This young man was fresh out of school, and quite nervous. This astoundingly gorgeous creature was causing him to perspire and was interfering with his concentration.

As he was beginning to examine her teeth, he felt a hand lightly surrounding his testicles. Being quite flustered and confused about her intentions, he said, "Young Lady, do you realize you have your hand near my scrotum?"

She smiled genially and said, *"Yes, Doctor. We're not going to hurt each other are we."*

There was a long pause. I handed Robbie the pen, and for once I did something right. I said nothing.

The antique grandfather clock in the foyer gonged six times. The ticking sounded like someone hammering a piece of iron.

One minute passed, two minutes.

I began to assemble materials and return them to my briefcase. I closed my briefcase and stood up.

"I've got a plane to catch Robbie."

"Dammit"

He signed the agreement. I gave him his copy.

"Thanks Robbie. I'll call you tomorrow."

The next morning, I stopped by headquarters and gave the agreement directly to the Corporate Attorney, Bob Maples, as he had requested. He said he would make copies and distribute it.

Bob was surprised that I had succeeded. I think the reason for the success was that I would have felt the same whether or not Robbie signed. A decision was being made so that we could move forward. Robbie probably sensed this. This situation was a slight variation of the Gerry Weinberg's *"Ninth Law of Pricing, The Principle of Least Regret,"* as found in his book, THE SECRETS OF CONSULTING.

Yes, Bob and I had the steak dinners, shrimp cocktail, wine, etc.

Croddy bounced my expense accounts.

A year later, Robbie was getting several thousand dollars per month in royalties.

I was "promoted" back to the field for a special assignment. I left the Corporation and stated my own consulting business two years later.

Another comment from William L. Livingston's book, HAVE FUN AT WORK:

> *"Rule — When the mess hits the fan, make sure you left a year ago."*

CHAPTER 4

THE THREE BUTTON PHONE

The financial/securities data base was updated every night. The opening, high, low and closing prices from the stock exchange were captured on magnetic tape. Data was transmitted from the tape via standard phone lines to an operations center in a distant city. This information was put on a National Time-Sharing system for remote access from typewriter style terminals at our customers' offices. The tape was not edited nor information produced for additions, deletions or changes, such as a cross reference file for ticker symbol changes.

I had been in the new project administrators position for three days. I was at work at 6:30 AM to see if the data transmission went smoothly and to put messages on the system if there were problems. I was unaware that the tape wasn't thoroughly edited for deletions or changes.

Around 8:00 AM, all three buttons on my phone lit up, all with the same problem. Investment bankers were missing millions of dollars from their portfolios. I handled the calls sequentially for about an hour, telling everyone I would call back as soon as the problem was solved. The sales force was also screaming!

I could not solve the problem answering the telephone. I had to get on the computer. When two of the lines finally opened, I picked up the phone, called the other extension, and put myself on hold. When I finished the third line, I called Rollie, who was down the hall, and told him to put me on hold and leave me there. All three buttons blinking on my phone.

I went to the computer room and found that the securities identifier, the ticker symbol SOJ had been changed to XON and discovered, for the first time, that we could not automatically change the ticker symbols in the users' portfolios. I broadcast a message over the network and started looking for other similar problems. This took about a half an hour.

About this time, Richie Greenman looked in my office and saw all three lines blinking. Our venerable, somewhat mercuric, Director of Applications Development went down the hall to ask Rollie what the hell was going on. All the buttons on Rollie's phone were also blinking and he could not be found. Apparently, the Branch Managers couldn't get to me, and Rollie had held them off for a while. Rollie decided the problem would get solved, but he wanted to be sure that Corporate management was fully aware of these kinds of problems. So they called Richie; Richie was not happy.

He came down to the computer room and in a tone that was a little too demanding, asked what was going on. I just gave him a blank look and said, "Damned if I know. I've only been here three days."

Richie just looked at me and turned beet red with anger. However, he decided not to pursue the issue, shrugged, and stalked away. He could tell that things were under control, at least temporarily. He probably recognized that he had been had by "Rollie and Johnny."

I spent the rest of the day making phone calls and the rest of the week finding people and methods of handling the present problems with a weak data base.

At this point, I thought about the four horseman of applications/project development:

1. Conceived in Confusion
2. Born into Ignorance
3. Developed in Chaos
4. Death by Neglect

It looked as though this project was just entering step Four.

The long term objective was to develop a human engineered application set and hold on to our present customers. It took about nine months to turn a messy situation around and in about fifteen months, we had a viable, growing product. We were using two sources for the data base and a very competent third party vendor that had good programs and maintained a quality data base.

And Vice Versa:

One thing that seems peculiar to
The problems of the hour:

The folks who know just what to do
Are not those with the Power.

S. S. Biddle

CHAPTER 5

NEW PRODUCT RELEASE

A new division had been formed and was in existence for about a year. The software product line was weak. The primary methodology for future growth was to use third party vendors with a good product, related knowledge and good support services.

This required complicated contract negotiations, evaluations, coordination with internal resources and the right people to administer the various projects. Pricing, which is the crabgrass of development, was also an important consideration. If there was more than one vendor to deal with, the problems grew exponentially.

The third party vendor was typically an independent entity or a small business employing less than 25 people. Our corporation was a large bureaucracy, fraught with politics, egos, and the like.

In the previous vignettes "The Brochure" and "Contract Re-Negotiation," there is some background for this story.

Some programs with origins at local offices were being used throughout the country. Some of the programs were acceptable, although undocumented. Most were causing problems, because of poorly disciplined implementation and the customers demanded more support. To solve this problem, the programs generating the highest revenue were put on one "National" system and support *attempted* from a central source.

This did not work. The "National" system had to be further cleaned and the scope of applications narrowed. Quality had to be the first priority to establish credibility with the sales force. Quantity and diversity would follow. Our friends, Richie and Rollie, in the newly formed applications development department, agreed on this as the primary objective. Rollie needed help and I ended up working in this scenario. I questioned my sanity several times.

What I found, (and Rollie had warned me) was a set of data bases and programs that were completely out of control. They were poorly maintained and the original sources were either not available nor reliable. The programs that processed the data were barely adequate and required a lot of training for the end user.

As usual, Corporate Management was impatient and expected us to magically cure about four years of poorly implemented applications. The National Time-Sharing system was indeed an odoriferous toxic waste dump for computer applications. (One situation describing a sample of this activity is in the story "The Three Button Phone.")

The need to get good products developed, tested, documented, etc. was crucial. Richie pushed us very hard to accelerate the development cycle, and Rollie and I had to fight tooth and nail with him. We had to continually point out that the hasty implementations of the past were the source of most of the present problems.

Richie was a good marketer. He was under a lot of pressure from the parent company and the VP of Marketing to get applications developed. That pressure, of course, came down the line to us, and Rollie was one of those tough technical types that wouldn't cave in to these kinds of pressures.

However, if really forced, he made sure that the results would not come back to us and drain our limited resources. That's another story! At times, we thought we would both be fired. Sometimes, we hoped we would be.

We had a good vendor for the data base product. We were looking at about six months to bring the product to market, and we were slightly ahead of schedule. The product was to be formally released on October 1. We had already moved the announcement date up from November 1.

Richie came to us and told us to rewrite the marketing release letter and move the date up another month. I gave him a look. It conveyed, "You are from outer space." Richie had been badgering us, and getting more unreasonable. His harsh demands resided some distance from reality.

I saw Rollie start to tense up. I thought he was about to tell Richie no in so many words, probably too many. But then Rollie said, "Okay Richie, what ever you say." Richie gave Rollie a strange look before he said, "Thanks," and left.

Now, I had known Rollie for about five years. I gave him a very suspicious look. I was surprised that he didn't give Richie hell. I had already argued about this issue with Richie on an almost daily basis. There was no way we would be ready a month earlier, and I was annoyed!

"Rollie, that is my product. How the hell can you commit it a month earlier? Now my ass is in the breeze!"

"John, calm down. Rewrite the release letter for *September 30* instead of *October 1*. September is a month earlier than October, isn't it?"

When the letter was sent, we were both surprised that Richie did not react. The memo went out and nothing was ever said.

> *"All human error is impatience, a premature renunciation of a method, a delusive pinning gown of a delusion."*
>
> Franz Kafka

II. THE FIELD

Good management protects the workers from the corporate bureaucracy.

CHAPTER 6

THE HAIRY ARM THEORY

The following is an old story, an old ploy used in every industry. However, it is a lot more fun being on the inside watching it happen.

We had a very competent salesman in our office, Charlie Sharpseller, who could sell anything to anybody. Charlie had put together a unique set of slides that he used in his prospect presentations. Along with Charlie's glibness, questioning strategies, and competence, he was a national top performer every year.

When the sales plan came out each year, most of the salesmen would moan and groan, cry and weep, wail and whimper, and plead their cases for quota reductions and territory changes. Charlie would take a couple of days off, read the sales plan carefully, sit down with management and logically resolve any quota and territory change problems. His typical remark was that "there is nothing wrong with a quota problem that a little selling won't solve." Charlie typically attained 100% of quota before the year was half over.

There was a high number of Marketing Managers. Individuals were promoted to Marketing Manager status from a sales position. Typically, they were on a fast track and would move on in a few months to staff positions or to special assignments for national accounts. Of course, each new Manager would review Charlie's slides and make suggestions for changes. They had to justify being a manager somehow, right?

Charlie had been offered Marketing Manager positions but refused them. "I don't want to manage people like me," he said. He was a salesman and enjoyed it.

We also had a customer engineer named Chester Stoleski. Chester was an excellent CE. However, Chester was the hairiest, swarthiest, toughest looking individual you ever saw. He looked more like an enforcer with his hair slicked back, penetrating dark brown eyes and hair crawling out of the collar and cuffs of his white shirt.

Chester was actually a prince. He was gentle, productive, competent, intelligent and humorous. However, his first impression was somewhat shocking. When a manager would call him at an installation and ask him when he would be finished, he would respond, "I could get done a lot sooner if I didn't have to talk on the phone."

Where does Chester fit into this story, you ask?

Charlie Sharpseller became frustrated with the "green Marketing Managers" constant screwing around with his presentation. Charlie made a flip chart with some important information on it and took a picture to make a slide out of it. The slide included Chester's arm and hand, with his index finger pointing at an item on the flip chart. His shirt sleeve was rolled halfway up his hairy forearm, which also had an ugly scar. Charlie put this slide in about a third of the way through the presentation. Chester said, by the way, that he got the scar when a card collating machine attacked him.

Whenever Charlie did his obligatory slide showing to a new Marketing Manager, he would insert this slide. When the slide appeared, the Manager would jump all over it and tell Charlie that it was inappropriate. Charlie was a good actor. He would look surprised and hurt. Charlie, ignoring the fact that the new Marketing Manager was referring to the "hairy arm," asked the Marketing Manager why the information on the flip chart wasn't appropriate. The marketing manager pointed out that the information was okay but that the hairy arm pointing at it was ugly and obscene. Charlie would argue vociferously that there was significant information on the chart, integral to the presentation and that Chester's arm wasn't that bad. The discussion would go back and forth for some time. Charlie would eventually give in to the manager and remove the slide.

I was a trainee when I first saw Charlie's slide presentation. A few months later he had a viewing for a new Marketing Manager. The slide was in there again! I noticed that there were more observers in the room. It seems that part of the office entertainment was watching Charlie finesse a new Marketing Manager. The Managers reaction and the ensuing argument was almost the same as the first time I saw it. Being young and naive, I was a little confused.

I asked Charlie why he put the slide in again. He then told me that he hasn't ever had to change his presentation. Every one of the Managers got upset with the "hairy arm" and insisted that he remove it. Charlie, of course, always argued with them and pointed out that there was important information on the flow chart. He would, very reluctantly, accede to the wishes of the Manager. The rest of the presentation was usually approved without question.

Charlie said:

> *"This is called the 'Hairy Arm Theory.' You should always provide a hairy arm for anybody looking for one."*

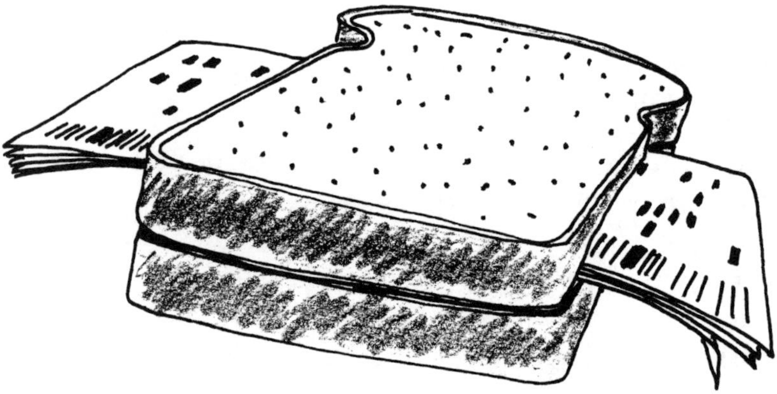

CHAPTER 7

WHAT ARE YOU HAVING FOR LUNCH?

At the time of medieval, but not ancient, history of computers, there was an installation that was changing from pre-generation one (the world of unit record machines, punched card media, tub files and rooms full of keypunch operators) to generation two (the world of the transistorized, stored program computer world). This was a tumultuous time when advancing technology was violently changing the social and hierarchal structure of corporations.

A machine that was feeding in punched cards that were output generated from a computer was having trouble reading the cards. The customer engineer (fixit man) was checking out the feed mechanism by feeding many cards through the reader portion of this device.

In those days, there were extension racks for the cards that would hold about 5000 cards, stacked one on top of the other, like slices of bread in a loaf. There was great pressure in the department to get this device running, but it was also lunchtime. The customer engineer thought he had the device working. He put a final stack of about 2000 cards in the rack and began to run them through the reader. He was also eating a very gooey peanut butter sandwich at the time. He put half of this sandwich on top of the stack of cards while he munched on the other half, not such an unreasonable thing to do, considering the card reader read only about 100 cards a minute. However, the card reader jammed again, and of course, the customer engineer looked under the machine cover while cycling the reader to check clearances. He picked up some more cards, and without looking, placed them in the rack, thereby sandwiching his sandwich between the stacks of cards in the rack.

Meanwhile, the computer room personnel were interrupting him frequently and asking when the machine was going to be fixed. These cards were read by wire contacts on an 80 x 12 copper contact matrix. In this case, the reader finally started cycling the cards through the machine properly, but of course the machine suddenly stopped. The matrix suddenly became an 80 x 12 gooey, peanut butter-copper non-conductor.

This story is not over.

The order taker (that's what the sales reps were called in those years), had been trying to get the Data Processing Manager and Division President to go to an Executive Meeting in an exotic location provided by the computer vendor. This was a situation in which customer executives were placed in an environment so that they could be appropriately brainwashed about the vendors capabilities, perceived or real. They were finally scheduled to go to the Meeting. The DP Manager had just been told that the meeting was cancelled on very short notice, and he had to explain to the Division President why there was a disruption in the Schedule.

On this particular afternoon, the order taker and the technical policemen (That's what the Systems Engineers were called in those years), happened to call on this particular DP manager. Both were unaware of the previous situations.

Can you imagine the Scenario? We walked into the DP Manager's office, the sales rep all aglow, thinking that he finally had his high level customer personnel scheduled for an Executive Seminar and totally unaware of hardware problems in the computer room.

The abnormally colored complexion of the DP manager alerted the sales rep that something was amiss! (He was one of the brighter ones who had an amazing grasp of the obvious!) The DP manager asked us what the hell kind of an outfit we worked for? What the hell kind of meetings do you schedule, then cancel? What the hell kind of repair people did we hire? What the hell am I supposed to tell the President? The plant managers were going to be all over his tail because of a blankety-blank-blank peanut-butter sandwich, etc. etc. After about five minutes of berating the Company, us, God, Congress, the railroads and the rest of the world, the DP Manager stopped to take a breath. I noticed that the armpits of his shirt were wet down to his belt and his glasses were steamed over. His eyes were not really tearing, they were sweating.

The sales rep, looking very confused, said, "I'll be glad to help, if you will just tell me, specifically, what is wrong." I was going to suggest we go out for coffee. After another few minutes of an octave higher harangue, I left the sales rep and DP Manager to their high-level misunderstanding and went to the computer room to try to decipher the peanut butter sandwich problem, which at the moment, sounded like the most important one.

The machine had been fixed and the customer engineer was

nowhere to be seen. However, the cool, calm operations manager (are there any other kind?) told me about the reader-sandwich problem. It took him and a couple of operators at least 10 minutes to tell the story. Every two words were punctuated by hysterical laughter. After we all calmed down, he said, *"It probably would have been fixed sooner if everybody left the repair guy alone."*

Well, as usual, we recovered. A few weeks later, even the Data Processing Manager saw the humor in our situation.

The customer engineer came to the office the next morning to find that some charitable soul had placed a peanut butter sandwich in his mailbox. I wonder who did that?

CHAPTER 8

THE NEW COMPUTER HAS A BUG!

When the third generation computers first came out, there were myriad problems, mostly software related. However, the following is the story of an unknown data communications link.

The new computer was placed in the new computer room, with the raised floor, proper environmental conditioning for temperature and humidity. It was surrounded by glass enclosed offices so that programmers and managers could look at this magnificent status symbol. The decor was blue and white. What else?

After the initial shakedown, the computer seemed to be operating properly, with expected problems encountered and dealt with. However, the "machine check" light would frequently come on and bring everything to a screeching halt. Needless to say, the computer would have to be restarted and the applications rerun. After several weeks, the local field engineers still could not find the problem. The people from the plant were called in. They ran extensive tests, and stayed with the computer around the clock for several weeks. The only thing that could be determined was that the computer failed more during the day than it did on the second shift. The position of the machine check in the random access memory was variable. The entire RAM core planes were replaced. The cable circuitry, terminations and connections were checked. Still the error would not go away.

During one of the testing periods between midnight and 6:00 AM, the problem was discovered. Two field engineers were running diagnostic programs. One was sitting at the console, the other went in one of the offices to make a phone call. A lot of pizza was consumed at this location. He dialed "9" and saw the machine check indicator turn on. There were no direct telecommunications attachments on this machine. The field engineer at the console asked the other field engineer to re-dial the telephone to see if the machine check light would come on again. Machine check again! They tried it with several telephones. Some caused a machine check, some didn't. On those that did, dialing "9" caused the machine check.

The phone company was called, the circuits traced through the cabling that ran *under the raised floor*. There was excess phone cable that was *coiled up directly under the Central Processing Unit of the computer*. When "9" was dialed, the "transformer effect" generated enough of a magnetic field to cause the machine to halt. The coil could not have been better placed.

The excess coil was re-routed and placed in a corner of the computer room. The problem went away. This problem existed for six months and was finally found — by chance!

What can be learned from this? When all known internal possibilities have been exhausted, look for external circumstances, logical and illogical, probable and ridiculous.

Check the environment.

CHAPTER 9

THE SECOND LAST ANNUAL

The branch office was going to have a Christmas Party. It was called the "Second Last Annual." The reason for this name will become obvious. Read on.

I was the newest Applied Science Rep-Trainee hired in the fall of that year. When I heard hushed tones about the "Second Last Annual," I inquired about it. "Shh," I was told.

"We don't talk about it within the walls of the office." Announcements of the "Second Last Annual" were passed by oral tradition and found under windshield wipers. The time and place were the only information on the sheet, along with phone numbers to call, after 7:00 PM, for further information.

It seems that the "First Annual Christmas Party" was tacitly approved by the Branch Manager. The notice, posted on the office bulletin board, gave the time and place with the suggestion that each person bring $5.00 for food and their own soft drinks. As you probably know, IBM was very opposed to any of the personnel consuming alcoholic beverages or engaging in any other immoral behavior at any function remotely related to company activities. There were even stories about the dangers of cashing your paycheck in a tavern.

The results of the "First Annual" were somewhat devastating. The most serious were three divorces and two pregnancies. (I don't know which divorces were related to which pregnancies.) The result was an edict by the Branch Manager that no informal parties of any kind would be announced, posted, discussed, mentioned or even thought about on company premises. As a matter of fact, he strongly suggested that there be no informal parties and declared the *"First Annual"* as the *"First and Last Annual."*

I called the number for information on the "Second Last Annual." It cost $20.00. I was to bring myself and a sleeping bag. Food and "beverages" would be provided. The reason for the sleeping bag was that if the party ran late, I could sleep at the party location and not have to drive home. Drinking was not mentioned.

This was a group of people that worked very hard and played very hard during the 1960s. They were a talented, dedicated, caring and helpful group of hell raisers. Here are a couple of the many experiences at the "Second Last Annual."

The "Second Last Annual" was not nearly as devastating as the first. There were no pregnancies and only one divorce. One of the guys, Fred, left the party and was very drunk. We tried to get him to stay, but he insisted on leaving. About 10 minutes later we heard a horn honking. We went out on the porch. It was cold and snowing like hell. Fred's car was sitting at the 4-way flashing red signal and the car behind him was blowing the horn. We ran down to the corner, and there was Fred, asleep, with his foot on the brake. We opened the door quickly and popped the gear shift into neutral. We moved Fred over, parked his car, kept his keys, and carried him back to the party.

Another person, Larry, had a lot to drink and left the party. We found out later that he lost control of his car and skidded into the middle of a field. He was not hurt and the car was not damaged. He had "barfed" all over the inside of his windshield. He turned on the wipers to clear the windshield and couldn't understand why he could not see. He left the car and found his way home, which was about a mile away. He was lucky he didn't freeze to death.

The next day, he went back for the car with the towing company. Naturally, the expulsions from his peristaltic reversals of the previous night were in a neatly frozen crystalline and chunk form on the windshield and dashboard of the car. He scraped and cleaned as much as he could, then started the car. Some of the "barf" had gone down the defrosters. He took the car to his friendly local mechanic and had the defroster tubing replaced.

Larry had more deodorizers in his car than the guys that cleaned out septic tanks. Nobody ever rode with Larry to go to lunch. The car smelled okay as long as you didn't turn on the fan for heating or cooling. Larry traded the car on a beautiful spring day when driving with the window down was ideal. The dealer called him about a week later and said unkind things to Larry. The car looked okay and was in great mechanical condition, but the dealer had to put it on the wholesale market.

Yes, a lot of humorous things happened at this and succeeding "Last Annuals." However, after these experiences, "Last Annuals" required depositing the car keys with someone responsible at the party.

Probably, the most important thing that happened, was the team building that went on. Perhaps we did not realize it at the time, but great ideas and suggestions came out of the "Last Annuals" just before quotas and territories were assigned.

I was promoted right after the "Eighth Last Annual." I think they are at about the "Thirtieth Last Annual" now.

CHAPTER 10

MANAGEMENT WISDOM

There just has to be some commentary on the limited vocabulary of most managers and their overuse of cliches. You might want to take this list with you to the next meeting and check off which ones are used. Maybe you will hear some new pearls of wisdom to add to the list!

Management Cliches (a few)

Choices:

know which side your bread is buttered on

sink or swim together

stand up and be counted

fighting in the trenches

go eyeball to eyeball

fight tooth and nail

bite the bullet

Colors:

green with envy

bull seeing red

purple with rage

pink with embarrassment

feeling blue

Cooperation:

ducks lined up

on the right track

getting up a head of steam

pulling his oar with the rest of the crew

playing our cards right

leave no stone unturned

nail down the facts

don't upset any applecarts

put your best foot forward

don't get trapped in a corner

taking the bull by the horns

keep your nose to the grindstone

put your shoulder to the wheel

keep your ear on the ground

Did you ever try to get a job done by *getting up a head of steam, putting your best foot forward, staying out of corners while taking the bull by the horns, keeping your nose to the grindstone, your shoulder to the wheel and ear on the ground?*

Try working in that position! Oh, well....

Cliches should be avoided like the plague!

CHAPTER 11

MANAGEMENT EGO

This is an interesting story about the involvement of two managers. The first manager, who I will call Sam, was one of those excellent managers. You know, one of the half dozen managers that have been very good throughout an individual's career. I will call the second manager Dorf, for obvious reasons. He is the type of manager you or I have been involved with for most of our careers. There are some other players, a Salesman, a Systems Engineer, and a Customer Engineer. All three of these individuals were very competent, even the Salesman. Of course, let's not forget the Customer, the one that Dorf appears *least* interested in.

In the early stages of the IBM 360 series computers, the mid 1960s, there were a lot of pressures on everyone and not enough resources to make these computers operate properly. In general, the hardware was reliable, but the systems software should have been relegated to some sort of a reversal of the conception and birth process.

I was the Systems Engineer on the account and had primary responsibility for coordinating program development with customer personnel for appropriate implementation of a customized operating system. We developed this custom operating system in a joint venture with some other aerospace companies for the purposes of time sharing usage on typewriter style terminals operating at 15 characters per second. Other applications were the development of utilities such as an I/O processor (tape to card, tape to printer, card to tape, etc.) for larger computers, and "background batch" processing for program development and non-time critical processing.

This entire project took about 17 months. Included were five programmers at the primary customer location, three Systems Engineers from different locations, project coordinators and programmers from other Aerospace Companies. Development activity proceeded satisfactorily. We were only about two weeks behind schedule when the computer arrived. It took about two weeks to unpack, install and do the *standard* operating system setup and *standard* hardware setup checkouts on the computer. We had been off-site at "Test Centers" and validated most of the custom software routines for the time sharing module.

During the final stages of testing, prior to turning the system over to the customer so that the *significant* monthly lease payments could start, we had some problems with the Telecommunications Control Unit (TCU), an IBM 2701. We had one terminal that would not work and when connected, caused a system "crash."

Of course, we were immediately told by Dorf that it was the software. We asked that a Customer Engineer at least look at the TCU while we reviewed the software. Dorf said that no, it could not possibly be the equipment because it had passed the *standard* checkout. I called the Salesman and described the situation. After about a week, a customer engineering trainee was sent and everything was okay with the *standard* testing for the "usual" TCU setup. However, I looked over his shoulder to see where the cables were connected at the TCU for the time sharing terminals.

We then went through more software tests, disconnected an offending terminal at the user's location and everything went fine. We connected a working terminal and associated cable where we had disconnected the allegedly offending terminal and cable, It also failed. So this isolated the problem back at the TCU. I called Ray, the Customer Engineer who was the expert on telecommunications devices. I told him about the problem, and asked him if he would come to the customer location if I could get it cleared with Dorf. Ray said he thought it was a minor problem and would be glad to help. However, Ray told me that, unfortunately, Dorf would not let him leave his present activities. Ray offered to help without letting anyone know. I vetoed this. It would get the wrong people off the hook and get both of us, especially Ray, in trouble. It was time to let the pressure build.

Well, hope springs eternal, so I tried the standard approach again. I called Dorf.

"Hey, Dorf. We disconnected a terminal, put one in that was working in place of the suspected one, and it failed too."

"You are not supposed to connect or disconnect anything. That's our job, fix your software."

"Hey, Dorf. We were just trying to help. We know how short you are on manpower. The problem still seems to be with the TCU. Ray is an expert on these devices. Please let him spend a half day helping us."

"Ray doesn't work in that territory," Dorf said. "I can't spare him from the other accounts. I can't spare anyone. I can't have my CE's working on problems generated by non-standard IBM systems software. Fix your program, the hardware is okay."

"Bye, Dorf."

At this point, the customer Systems Programming Manager, Jack, asked me to have a drink and supper with him after work. I guess he noticed the deep fingernail marks in the palms of my hands, the result of my tightly clenched fists. Over dinner, we talked about "the problem." Jack was an "old timer" from the world of punched card equipment, first and second generation computers and now the wonderful world of telecommunications in the third generation. He was an excellent manager and knew how to solve problems. He was also well known for being unorthodox. His boss, the very powerful VP of Information Services, valued Jack, and supported and protected him from the highly structured and autocratic establishment types. I told Jack that I was going to press my Branch Manager to help with this problem.

After our good meal at a local mafia owned and operated restaurant, we decided on a course of action.

"We want to be sure we have full management attention from all quarters," Jack said.

"What do you suggest?"

"Do you know where the cables are in the TCU?"

"Yes."

"Do you know how to take them out and switch them?"

"Yes"

"Let's go."

We went back to the location, powered down the TCU, and at Jack's suggestion, I switched the offending cable with another connection, that had never failed. By the way, it was now 1:00 AM.

"We didn't do anything, right?"

"Yes, good night, Jack."

"Goodnight."

The next day when the terminal users came in to start their work, guess what? Operations got a call from a powerful, ill tempered, middle management user, who was not an IBM proponent and whose terminal had not failed since installation. He did not route his complaint through the data processing department, but called the sales rep directly. The guerilla warfare from the night before worked.

Well, it sort of worked. Never underestimate the narrow minded assemblage of ego, ignorance and incompetence of management. The sales rep called Dorf. Dorf called me.

"I told you to fix your software."

"The software has not been changed. It has to be the TCU."

"It's the software."

"Talk to the sales rep. You are the one holding up the beginning of the monthly payments."

"It's your responsibility."

"Bye, Dorf"

I hung up before I made any comments about Dorf's personal

hygiene, canine genetic heritage or the marital status of his parents at his birth.

At this point, the Salesman was called again. There is significant motivation here. The Salesman does not get the last 50% of his commission until the computer is turned over to the customer. I suggested that the plant be contacted. There had to be something that was non-standard with the TCU. The system had been working at the test centers. What was different here? *We obviously did not have local, available field engineering management with the desire* to solve the problem. I told the salesman that the customer and I could do nothing more. We had tested all the known options, isolated the problem and had the *tacit refusal* of the local CE manager to address it.

Nobody likes to call in the plant people and have his or her ignorance and incompetence exposed. Of course, it also costs the Branch Office a lot of money to ship people in from the plant. The Branch Office had already lost more than two weeks of revenue amounting to several thousand dollars. An important, noisy management level user has not been operational for two days. *The pressure is on!*

Now, I'm starting to have some fun. Everybody else is sweating just as much as I am.

Sam, the marketing manager called me. He asked me to come into the office to meet with Dorf. I made only one request. Dorf, for his own safety, should be kept out of arm's reach. Sam assured me of this and firmly requested that I "cool it."

Dorf, Sam, and I met in Sam's office. Note the turf location. Dorf articulated some pious procedural platitudes while I remained silent with an attitude of rigorous reality. Dorf was a clear example of *"Structure and Protocol as a Crutch for the*

Incompetent." Sam stood up, and requested that we all remain standing, because this problem was going to be solved in a hurry.

Sam looked at Dorf and said, "Look, no finger pointing. How can we get this system up?"

"Fix the software. It can't be the hardware."

I did not say anything.

"We don't fix software problems, just hardware," Dorf continued.

I was not about to get into the old "my software, your hardware" squabble. I just smiled.

"Sam, I received my check today. I am sure Dorf has his too. Here is mine. Dorf, give your check to Sam. If it is software you get both checks. If it is hardware, I get them both."

Sam just looked at Dorf.

After a long pause, Dorf said, "You know that gambling on the premises is against company policy. I could turn you in."

"That's my job, Dorf," Sam snapped.

At this point, Sam gave me my check back and said, "That was a poor way to make your point. Dorf, can you send Ray to the customer first thing in the morning to check out the hardware? If not, let's call the plant right now."

Dorf's blood pressure was obviously up. He just nodded and left the office. I was wondering if I should use a "Youngstown Special" to start my car.

Sam looked at me and smiled. "Thanks," he said. "That took a lot of guts, but you better be right or we both hang."

The next morning, Ray was at the location and told me how surprised he was that Dorf let him come over. In less than an hour, he found a terminator, a jack, about the size of your small fingernail, and removed it. He re-assembled the cables. We tested the system and it was fine.

Ray looked at me with a very steady gaze. "I noticed that the cables were not installed in the proper sequence," he said. "I re-sequenced them."

Unfortunately, he made this statement in front of Jack and me at the coffee machine. I made the mistake of looking at Jack. We both just cracked up laughing.

"So that's why you put Dorf against the wall with your paycheck routine," he said. "You knew you couldn't lose. But, don't worry, I'll never tell."

Ray apparently had as much respect for his boss as we all did.

Jack and I took Ray to lunch and filled him in on the guerilla warfare. Ray took great delight in our attempt to educate Dorf. Ray was very mature, quiet and seldom said anything negative. However, he did describe Dorf as having the "deadly combination of mental constipation and anal retentivity."

I waited one day. I called Dorf and sincerely thanked him for his cooperation in solving the problem. I told him I understood that we were all under pressure and hoped things would be more congenial in the future. He responded, somewhat weakly and without enthusiasm, that he hoped so too. Shortly after that he was promoted out of field operations to a staff job at another location.

The Salesman took my wife and me out for a night on the town.

I thanked Sam for his help. He suggested I go to charm school, but then decided that it probably wouldn't work.

The Customer asked for more Systems Engineering assistance on the account. The Salesman said he would give him another Systems Engineer and two trainees if he could have me for another account. The Customer refused. Now, I had to get my ego in check! It was one of the nicest compliments I ever received.

Comment: Problems get solved by people who operate outside of the standard policy box. The Systems Manager, The Systems Engineer, the Customer Engineer by their actions, (of Commission or Omission) got the job done. Management did not solve it until pressed. If one sticks strictly to policy, *very little gets accomplished!*

Questions:

How did the problem(s) get solved?

What should or could have been handled differently?

Where were the points of communication breakdown?

Who played you bet your job?

What were the agendas of the various players?

What would you have done?

Pick each player and speculate about how you would operate.

CHAPTER 12

THE SYSTEMS PROGRAMMER

In a long-term information systems implementation, there was a systems programmer of the highest caliber. Wilbur was short, slender, about 5'6", wore round glasses and appeared to be very unassuming. He was a lot like "Mr. Peepers" or a Methodist Minister. Wilbur was the principle systems programmer in the installation referenced in the "Ego and Ignorance" Chapter of this book.

When he asked questions, he would start with the basics. Is it plugged in? Is it turned on? Are the cables connected?, etc. He also had several very insightful litanies for isolating and solving problems very quickly in complicated systems programming scenarios.

Wilbur's own systems programming was impeccable. His programming was more a work of art than a technical masterpiece. His coding would remind one of the smooth flow of a ballet dance, all perfectly coordinated. Everyone wanted Wilbur to work on their projects. He was not an arrogant elitist type that one too often finds in data processing departments. He was helpful, humorous and usually solved problems by generating a relaxing, non-threatening atmosphere.

Wilbur was also a social animal, not the odoriferous, unkempt, dandruff covered, sandaled hermit that was the classic image of the systems programmer. When we went on test trips, no matter what the work load, Wilbur found time for recreation. He was known to drive a convertible with the top down in a thunderstorm. On purpose, yet!

When it came to computers, Wilbur was top notch. However, Wilbur did have one area where he was dysfunctional. If he had to deal with something mechanical, strange things would happen to him. It wasn't that he couldn't understand mechanical objects or systems. He knew what to do. The devices would just misbehave in his presence.

For instance, we would not let him load cards in the card reader, continuous form paper in the printer, mount magnetic tapes on the tape drives, or load disk packs on to the disk drives. We wouldn't even let him touch the systems console on the computer! As a matter of fact, operations personnel became very nervous whenever he was in the data processing center. Needless to say, he was a great source of humor and took our jibing well. He could dish it out too, particularly when he looked at our programs.

We were all working late one night. In attendance were the programming manager, an applications programmer, Wilbur, the systems programmer, the operations manager and me. We decided to have some coffee. Do you know how many coin flips it takes to get the odd man to buy the coffee? You guessed it, Wilbur ended up buying the coffee.

We offered to put the coins into the coffee machine for Wilbur. He had a history of playing with this particular machine and losing. He had been seen negotiating with the machine before buying coffee. The vendor hated to see Wilbur come for refunds when the machine was being reloaded. We all waited anxiously as Wilbur dug the change out of his pocket. He insisted on putting the coins in for each of us—over our objections. There were some side bets on when the machine would fail. However, we each made our selection, got our coffee and breathed a sigh of relief.

After the four of us had our coffee, Wilbur put in coins for himself. The first time, *no cup dropped* and his coffee went down the drain. The second time, the cup dropped but *no coffee* was generated. The third time, the machine took his coins and then turned on the *"no more coffee"* light. We all laughed hysterically, including Wilbur!

I wonder where Wilbur is now. I'm sure he is not sitting at a Personal Computer keyboard. His typing speed was about 2 characters per minute. I am sure he is helping others become productive and letting someone else get the coffee.

III. CORPORATE TRAINING

Train for quality and service,

productivity will follow.

CHAPTER 13

SALESMEN AND "TECHIES"

During the transition years from punched card data processing to computers, there were some drastic changes in many corporate cultures. The advent of the Russian "Sputnik" satellite in October of 1957 and the great rush to sciences and landing on the moon in 1969, forced many organizations to change. These changes are still going on today.

At that time, there was a shortage of technical, engineering and scientific personnel in all disciplines. Corporations needed people with these skills in all areas—R&D, Engineering, Marketing and, of all places, Sales. The integration of direct logic from the scientific types into the sales environment was a challenge for most companies. Many organizations took the industry education route. This was effective, although at times it illustrated great ignorance. One of the worst travesties was trying to beat questionable sales dogma into scientifically oriented personnel.

At one industry school, the Applied Science Representatives were being introduced to relevant hardware and related applications. This particular school lasted about five weeks. At the same time, there was an "intermediate" sales school being conducted for sales representatives who had been with the organization for about a year. There was a lot of good natured interplay between the two groups. The salesmen would ask the "techies" to "say something to me in FORTRAN." The Applied Science Reps would ask them for tips on "expense account creativity."

The manager of the sales school came up with a bright idea. One Friday afternoon, he had the sales reps put on a little play. The theme of this 10 minute presentation revolved around some sales reps that quit the mother company to form their own competitive organization. The Applied Science Reps were required to sit in on this to provide an adequate audience, along with other members of the sales school and visitors.

About seven minutes into the play, while one of the "actors" was contemplating suicide and expressing great remorse about leaving such a fine organization, someone in the back of the group started humming—dum de dum, dum de dum, dum de dum de dum, dum dum dum, dum dum dum, dum de dum de dum, and of course, the rest of the group finished it off with the refrain: Mickey Mouse, Mickey Mouse, etc. The chorus was never completed. The manager of the sales school jumped to the stage and screamed to our manager, "Get the techies the hell out of here."

He had apparently forgotten one of Murphy's Laws.

"Disaster will occur when visitors are in the classroom."

The "techies" went back to the lecture hall. The instructor did not return for several minutes. Later, they found out that he was laughing so hard, it took him a while to compose himself. He hurriedly finished the lecture for the day, gave the assignment and dismissed the class early. He had to keep a straight face. At the local establishment that night, he confided that the response to the skit was a put down that the sales people needed in order to realize and deal with the new realities of the marketplace, as well as the internal changes within the corporation.

The next day, the manager of the educational facility, came in and reprimanded the group. The reprimand was not harsh. He pointed out the importance of the sales school and the confidence and support that the sales reps would need from the Applied Science Reps in the field. He was right, but he failed to realize that the intent was not vicious. He failed to realize that those with a technical mind-set prefer to deal with facts, focus on productivity, are unafraid to debate issues, and recognize propaganda.

These attitudes did not diminish the support given to sales. The Applied Science Reps just liked to keep the atmosphere honest. The interesting thing is that most of the Sales Reps thought it was "Mickey Mouse" too. But, they had to follow the program. It was probably a good thing that the sales school manager was not the manager of the Applied Science Rep School!

CHAPTER 14

THE RERUN

A few of the "Applied Science Representatives" who underwent a title change to "Systems Engineer-Scientific," and who had experience on large scale systems in the early 1960s, were invited to attend a week long industry school on the IBM 360 operating system. The product line had been announced and the computers existed only in test centers and a few early test "Beta" sites. The only early users were NASA and some other Government installations. The point is, it was very early in the game of a computer line announced earlier than intended and labelled a "paper tiger" by the competition. IBM got away with a lot of anti-trust-like-behavior that would not be tolerated today.

Joe McFeely and I were part of a group of about thirty "techies" who went to New York City. On our arrival, we checked into the hotel room after buying a six-pack at a local delicatessen. It was about 11 PM. We flipped through the TV channels and the only thing that was on was "The Blob." Even in 1964-65 this was a rerun. I think it was Steve McQueen's first movie. It was about this huge extra-terrestrial blob of protoplasm that absorbed everything in its path via its semipermeable membrane exterior for its own nourishment. A truly hokey flick! The Blob would make noises as it gobbled up everything in its path—"bloob, bleep, blopp, margle, sshullp," etc.

The next morning, we had breakfast and went to the data center for our first class. We knew some of the other fellows and reacquainted ourselves with them and discussed some of the political and technical aspects of the new computer line. Almost everyone had watched "The Blob" the previous evening. Some of the technical aspects and dietary choices of "The Blob" in the movie were also being humorously discussed.

Class started with us all introducing ourselves. The instructor was from the development lab in Poughkeepsie and had never worked in the field. He was a nice guy and very knowledgeable about the operating system "internals." The materials he handed out were copier generated detailed hardware specifications and related engineering programming structures that had obviously been hurriedly assembled. This material was about two levels too deep for what we needed to implement in the field. Joe was sitting in the row behind me. We just looked at each other and shrugged. The same reaction was observed among the other attendees.

The instructor started lecturing at 9:00. After about 15 minutes, he had lost most of the group. He was very nervous. He had obviously been pushed into this, probably by the marketing department. The material was not properly geared for field support "techies." We later found out that he was told one week before the class that he was going to teach it. There was just not enough time for preparation and generation of the appropriate classroom oriented materials.

We all sat and tried to follow the material. Very few questions were asked. The instructor appeared to be somewhat panicked and was just trying to get through the material. At about 10:15, some very quiet noises were heard from the row behind me. "Bloop, bleep, mrrp, frrrup, margle, blaap." It was Joe, illustrating his feeling that he was being absorbed by "THE BLOB." The class broke up laughing. The instructor looked bewildered and confused.

We suggested an early coffee break. Joe, a couple of other guys and I talked to the instructor during the break. We told him that everything was over our heads. We suggested that we "round table the room" and ask each other questions with the instructor as moderator. There was a pool of knowledge in the room that could be transmitted within the group. There were some of us that could sort out what was required. The instructor helped us when he understood what our needs were relative to field support and installation of the computers. To his credit, he responded very favorably to our suggestions, and in this atmosphere of cooperation, he contributed meaningfully. Many members of the class also presented to the rest of the group.

We spent the rest of the day and evening in discussion and reorganization of course materials. We drove the copy center crazy every morning with materials that we developed each night for the rest of the week. It turned out to be a very productive week. A few months later, we saw some of the materials we developed show up in the standard courses.

The instructor had called his manager and told him what was happening. One of the things that was the most gratifying was that management did not stick to an ego based hard line and insist that the course be taught as dictated. A couple of the education center people sat in on the class, helped us assemble information into a logical format and took a very proactive, positive attitude.

I am sure the reruns of this class were better that the reruns of "The Blob!"

Question: How was this class, destined for almost certain failure, turned into a success. Who were the people involved in making it successful? Why?

CHAPTER 15

INDUSTRY EDUCATION - LONG TERM

Many corporations involve some of their top field people in "schools" that can last several weeks or even months. Another Systems Engineer from our office and I attended one of these mental marathons in New York City.

The school had been described as an exercise where half the group of about 60 were chained to a desk with programming sheets and coding forms, fed cheese sandwiches, and whipped by the other half. At the mid-point of the program, the two groups switched roles.

A typical week consisted of classes for about six hours, doing research and working on computers for another 10 to 12 hours for six days. On Saturday night, we would involve ourselves in some diversions, plentiful in New York City.

On Sundays, we would ride bicycles in Central Park, visit the museums, etc. But by Sunday night, we were back in the books. It was a challenging and beneficial experience with some extremely talented people, both participants and instructors.

Steve and I were working on a set of "Black Box" problems

that were devised by a well known General Systems Theorist. We had figured out all but one of the systems and were spending an inordinate amount of time on it. I don't remember the details of the final problem, but the scenario was something to the effect that only *invalid* inputs were valid.

We were sitting in one of the local "Irish" bars where you could get a corned beef sandwich and a pitcher of beer for a reasonable price. On our stipend, we didn't hit spots like P.J. Clarks, MaMa Leone's etc. Anyway, Steve and I were thinking about this Black Box problem.

A couple of the other attendees came in for supper and went back to the school, the usual drill. It happened to be a weeknight, but we were so frustrated, we kept on drinking more beer. Our conversation covered a range of topics, but always came back to the "Black Box."

Steve's voice and laugh descended into a deep, sonorous, basso profundo that increased in volume in direct proportion to beer consumed. Some of the guys came back from the school at about 11 P.M., had a couple of drinks and left for the hotel. Again, this was the usual routine. Steve and I stayed and kept on discussing various issues.

Well, the relaxation technique worked. All of the sudden, Steve stood up and looked like he had been goosed by a vacuum cleaner. "I've got it!," he yelled. I immediately looked under table and said, "Got what?" Of course with the dumb look on my face, he roared loudly with laughter and we were thrown out of the place. I guess the bartender had warned us several times. The patrons were trying to watch a baseball game on the TV. Apparently, we were not part of "in crowd" at this particular establishment.

Steve wanted to go back to the school right away. I advised against it, based on our condition. We went back to the hotel and wrote down our approach. The next day, we tried our hypothesis of doing everything *invalid*. That was the answer.

One purpose of the exercise is obvious. See if you can make a system do what it is *not* supposed to do. Unfortunately, too often, we find these circumstances *after* the system is released to the customer or end user.

Questions:

What "Black Box" experiences have you had?

a) prevention

b) reaction

c) serendipity

The general answer to the above three items is good planning. Model building, testing, analysis and feedback all being part of *prevention*. If the environment is evaluated carefully, and significant, meaningful communication occurs during the development process, then it is much easier to *react* when unexpected events occur after implementation. *Serendipity* (unexpected benefits and realizations) usually occurs when there is a good planning, development and implementation process with good feedback from all the participants.

How do you train yourself to look *"Outside"* of a system?

Typically, one way to look outside of a system is to give the system invalid inputs and see how it responds. These responses will give a lot of insight into the quality of the system. Another approach is to compare it to other similar systems.

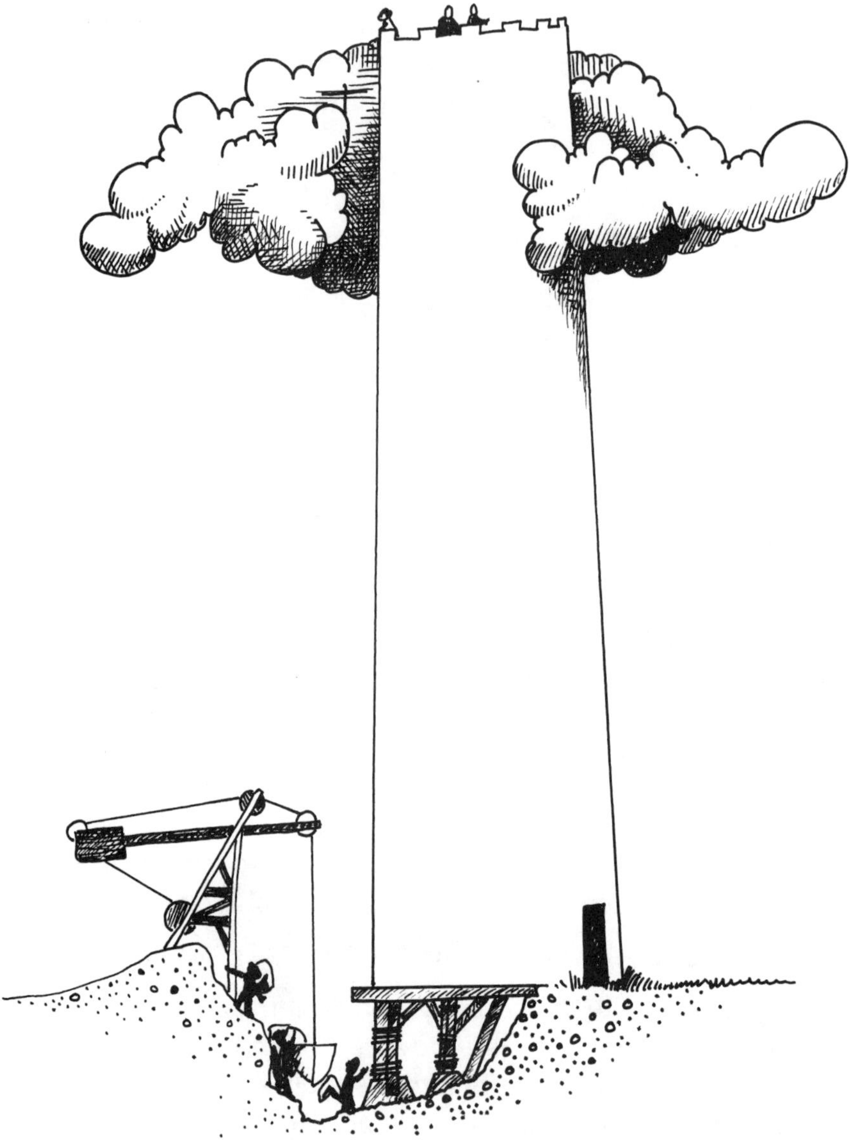

IV. INDEPENDENT CONSULTING

The independent consultant is the vehicle that assists organizations through environmental change.

CHAPTER 16

(The following, slightly modified, was published in the third quarter, 1978, issue of "The Independent," the newsletter for the Independent Computer Consultants Association (ICCA).)

THE INDEPENDENT CONSULTANT

Independent Consultants implement. They are not necessarily idea people or innovators. There are many people with ideas and innovative approaches. There are too few who really implement.

This situation exists particularly in corporations where there appears to be the syndrome of: "Who can I get to do my job so I won't have to get my hands dirty?" Many people in many corporations think that being an executive is a matter of ego, intimidation of peers, doing as little as possible, carefully watching for opportunities to take the credit for themselves and place the blame for mistakes on others. When we look at a corporation to see who is really producing, we will find that most of the meaningful productivity and implementation comes from an amazingly small percentage of the people.

It is usually from these ranks that Independent Consultants arise. They get disenchanted with trying to implement through an arbitrary, capricious bureaucracy and seeing their efforts diluted, polluted, substituted and themselves prostituted. So, they go into business for themselves.

Then the following happens. Their services are acquired by corporations, very often the ones they have left. They are now in the arena where the *willingness to commit and produce* are recognized. Independent Consultants are no longer in the position of many of their former peers, where as long as the members of the corporate herd are drawing a regular paycheck, they do enough to get by, let projects slip, and blame the subsequent problems on someone else. Somehow, the corporation becomes sensitive to, and appreciative of, the dollars they spend on an Independent Consultant to obtain the desired results that are nearly impossible to produce from the politically incestuous bowels of many corporations.

Another reason a corporation likes to use Independent Consultants is that they bring *fresh ideas and attitudes* to a company. Independent Consultants are typically in contact with many different types of businesses and people from the executive offices to the manufacturing floor. *They are seldom pretentious or arbitrary. They typically ask penetrating questions to help their clients perceive the definitions of requirements or recognize answers they already have.* They are independent of the emotional blocks to reason that exist within an organization.

A major consideration in using an Independent Consultant is the *resources in experience and knowledge* that a company may not have internally. The advent of microcomputers and their use by non-data processing professionals has created an incredible need for the application software designer, developer, and most of all, someone who can implement—all wrapped up in one person.

The need for special training requirements, interdepartmental coordination and walking the political tightrope with the client's data processing department are also requirements that can be met by an Independent Consultant. *The Independent Consultant who has a varied, technically oriented background, good communication and interpersonal relations, and an understanding of human engineering is well equipped for this environment.*

One of the major situations in the implementation of microcomputers is the excruciatingly slow process of convincing the data processing department that the Independent Consultant is complementing their service. What is occurring is the intrinsic development of distributed data processing in the organization without the company management recognizing it.

The Independent Consultant has a definite responsibility to "look ahead." This means looking at the installation of a microcomputer as a future node in a DDP (Distributed Data Processing) network. Even though it may not be discussed openly, the egg has hatched and it *will* evolve.

The Independent Consultant intelligently guides this evolution or similar ones until the client corporation needs and uses it. *The Independent Consultant executes externally driven intrinsic planning. They control their egos.* Eventually the client will perceive the results as revolutionary.

Perhaps, after all, a revolution is nothing more than perceived evolution.

In summary, the three major uses of an Independent Consultant are:

1. *Requirements Definition* (See Chapter 22)
2. *Implementation* (See Chapter 18)
3. *Long Range Planning* (See Chapter 19)

These three major activities are, of course, expanded in great detail in client engagements.

CHAPTER 17

CONSULTANT'S QUALITY CIRCLE

I started my own consulting business in 1975. After some tight finances, near disasters, and reaching the verge of bankruptcy, business took a turn for the better. A couple of clients emerged in the functional end user departments of corporations, rather than the standard, highly structured, elitist data processing departments.

One of these organizations was a small, and rapidly growing parts manufacturing, assembly, and distribution firm, selling principally to OEM (Original Equipment Manufacturers) customers. The primary problem was that they had difficulty keeping track of new business opportunities. The time from sales forecast to engineering definition, through design, customer approval, product pricing, etc. was usually several months. There was lack of customer follow-up as well as problems in the tracking of product development through the organization itself. Frankly, there was also a lack of commitment from the sales force and manufacturing representatives.

In a cooperative, open atmosphere with marketing management, we generated a system that logged target dates for the various activities. The reps were bird-dogged by District Sales Managers. The system was driven by a product quantity and estimated dollar sales forecast. Feedback from the internal activities such as design, sample building, testing, approval and submission was distributed to the District Sales Managers on a weekly basis. This was coordinated with engineering and product pricing. Armed with good customer specs and response, the sales force became more productive and manufacturing could get more accurate long term forecasts.

A couple of political statements should be made here. First, the President was committed and involved in this process. Secondly, there was about a 50% turnover in salesmen and manufacturing reps within the first six months of the reporting cycle. Many of the reps were making commitments, not meeting them, and screwing up in general. All of a sudden, the data processing department, along with many of the salesmen, were trying to figure out how such accurate information was being developed and implemented.

After about 5 years of operation, the sales tracking program that was on the small computer was moved to the mainframe. At that time, I suggested that it be redesigned for interrogatory processing, because the output being generated was getting voluminous and was not selective enough. Of course, the "mainframe gurus" were in a hurry and just took the design as it was and "mainframed it." They stopped running the program about four years ago. Nobody could use it because they had to sort through an inaccurate 200 page detail listing to get summary information.

There are many paths to this story. But, you will notice the title had something to do with a popular expression, *"Quality Circle."*

The quality circles within an organization are merely a set of functional procedures for generation of good feedback and good communication. *No magic!*

Relevant data encouraged people to communicate. Each project had a sequential series of activities and sign-offs to be accomplished. All the related departments had the project list. Everyone knew who was responsible at every stage of each project. The longest anyone had to wait to see the present status of a project was four days. If the project value was over a certain amount, you might even get a call from the President, who is basically a nice guy. He is capable, justifiably, of being an irrational son of a bitch when the job is not getting done.

The real quality circle to be mentioned is the long-term one. I did a lot of consulting work for this organization in several areas, always insisting that engagements go through a planning process. There are times that engagements were lost, because I would not get into fireman mode, along with sloppy implementation, just because someone was in a hurry. There was always a price to pay later to fix a hasty implementation, along with the perception that the consultant was holding a gun to the client's head.

There had not been a significant project with this client for about five years. They have gone through the typical PC scenario. End users, such as the District Sales Managers, have toughed it out, going through a process of self instruction and manual procedures to get their work done since the mainframe output had rendered itself useless. They are now at the stage where they have to operate more efficiently, integrate, reduce duplication of effort and get management information on a timely basis.

I received a call from the Sales Administrator. They need to manage the sales force and track projects again. The organization is still growing rapidly. Summary data cannot presently be assembled efficiently from disjointed Personal Computers that are geographically dispersed. The task is to get functional data acquisition and reporting back on track.

What is the real *"Quality Circle"* from the consulting standpoint? Always to do the job right. Plan. Get management involvement. Give good service after implementation. *You* might get a phone call *years* later, because *you* insisted on doing the job right!

"Things of Quality Have No Fear of Time."
Anonymous

CHAPTER 18

THE SKUNKWORKS

In addition to my consulting work, I do some teaching at a local Community College. This is a form of "psychic" income. This also provides a break from my regular activities as an Independent Consultant, and I enjoy teaching.

It is also an opportunity to dispel some myths for some people taking their first courses in data processing and computer literacy. Some of those myths are described in Chapter 25, *"So You Want to Buy a Computer?"*

When I was teaching one 16 week, Introduction to Data Processing course, one of the students came up to me and suggested that I go talk to his boss. Harry had a Ph.D. in Plant Physiology and worked at a biological and biochemical research facility in the "boonies." He was going to coordinate the computing development activities. He knew he needed help. This was his first computer course since taking a FORTRAN programming course as an undergraduate.

I called the Manager of the facility, Rolf Grutweig, and made an appointment to see him. It was late October. The facility consisted of a few large greenhouses connected to a small laboratory. The administration building was an aging house trailer that had been gutted and refurbished as a "temporary" office. A nearby farm house was being remodeled for offices.

Rolf also had a Ph.D. specialty in the biological sciences. The local staff consisted of four people with Doctorates, three more with BS degrees, an administrative assistant, two maintenance people and additional temporary help during the summer and fall when a lot of work was going on in the greenhouses and at the farm test plots. The dress was very informal. Sweatshirts, jeans, safety glasses, safety shoes and hard hats were the usual look. Rolf was a somewhat moody and recalcitrant chain smoker. He was a good manager and very knowledgeable about all facets of the research center, including the proper use of farm equipment.

The facility was about 60 miles away from the headquarter's bureaucracy. The environment was very creative and productive. Ideas were seldom rejected quickly. Rolf would probe and investigate an idea relentlessly, but efficiently. The discussions often became quite heated! Situations usually boiled down to resolution of allocation of resources. There was almost always a group consensus and placement of responsibility with the acceptance of an idea. Rolf made the remark that there were always many good ideas, but the problem was picking the one that would provide the proper approach and could be implemented.

The data acquisition, reduction and reporting capabilities were archaic and inefficient. The data was gathered manually in the greenhouses or at the farm test plots. The environment was hot or cold, wet or dry, and usually dirty. Pollen, perspiration, wind and recalcitrant writing instruments made transcription of data to the standard clipboard difficult.

Following this, the dog-eared data sheets with the smudges and shakily written entries had to be deciphered, reports formatted, averages manually computed, etc. Obviously, the opportunities for the introduction of errors were very great. The data was entered into a very rudimentary word processor, with no computational capability, on a low end microcomputer. The assembly of the research reports took about three weeks from the time the data was taken. If some numbers did not make sense, the memory recovery of the person that recorded the data for that particular experiment was not usually adequate. Many of the experiments had to be rejected.

Rolf had made many requests to the data processing group to either help him or allow him to purchase equipment. As usual, the data processing group did not understand the needs of a non-standard functional end user. The thought of losing control or power over someone by allowing them to purchase their own equipment was unacceptable to the standard, highly structured, narrow minded data processing bureaucracy. So, some empty promises were made and Rolf had been stonewalled for at least two years at this point.

Rolf had hidden the microcomputer in his budget and had also purchased some key driven data collectors. My mission was to set up the data collectors so that the information could be accurately assembled. It was an interesting development environment.

In the winter, the wind howled around that trailer. We all wore thick socks and long underwear. There were usually about four or five of us in the trailer at one time. Sometimes the trailer would not get above 60 degrees and that was from the waist up. When someone came in from outside, they would be verbally attacked if the door was open for more than a second!

The floor was drafty and had to be at 40 degrees. For lunch, we usually drove about eight miles into town to a McDonald's fast food franchise, ate slowly, and warmed ourselves.

The use of electronically keyed, highly reliable data collection, data transmission to a microcomputer, and expeditious report generation was accomplished over a six month time period. The reports were passed directly to other groups, such as product development via microcomputer to microcomputer using modems. The "DP" department was bypassed. The reports were usually generated within one working day from the time the data was taken. If there were any questions, the experiment was still set up so that any data inconsistencies could be resolved.

The data processing department looked at the Research Center and the Product Development group as using "toys." They did not realize the amount of experimental data that was residing on diskettes. This presented a huge information problem that they would have to sort out later.

The computing needs of the research center were increasing. There was a need to collect rainfall, soil and air temperatures, humidity, solar radiation and wind direction data for coordination with the farm test plot data. This involved setting up a small weather station and recording the information. The initial approach was to have a data recorder at the weather station that would print the readings on a strip printer. This data would be re-keyed later into the microcomputer that was already being used full time.

I suggested purchasing another computer to connect with the weather station. This way, with a phone line, we could "download" the data from the weather station and bypass an error prone re-keying cycle. However, the problem was that all computer purchases had to go through data processing.

> *"All organizations have their mavericks who find it necessary to conspire against norms in order to solve problems, and they play a crucial role in sustaining the corporation"*
>
> William L. Livingston

Very quickly, the weather station become very expensive. A several thousand dollar environmental controller and environmental protection casing was added to the original amount for the instrumentation and data collector. The word "computer" or "processor" or anything that suggested data processing equipment was not mentioned in the purchase order. For instance, the printer for the computer (environmental controller) was called a "mass environmental recorder." The plotter was called the "environmental graphing module." The purchase order, filled with confusing pseudo-scientific jargon, was approved without question. To ask questions would be to admit ignorance. This is one way to get around individuals who cover up their ignorance (stupidity?) with misplaced ego.

The new computer was hidden in what formerly was the bathroom of the remodeled farmhouse. If anyone from Headquarters arrived, the door was closed. They were usually escorted to the conference room at the other end of the "house." There was great levity regarding the location of the computer and that my first name is John.

The new computer was used to download collected data from the weather station every couple of days. The rest of the time it supported the research facility in many ways. We could do a significant amount of special purpose computation: bioassays, statistics, graphs, presentation materials, word processing, data file handling, and even uploading and assembling reports and data on the mainframe computer in the headquarter's data processing center.

With the data communications link, the data processing department did not know what was happening because the usage was low at first. Processing was being initiated from outside the standard operations activities in the data processing center.

By now, about a year and a half had gone by and the data acquisition and reporting was operating quite efficiently. Data was being assembled from the greenhouses, the laboratory, the weather station and many geographically dispersed test plots. However, the ever present information cycle was increasing in volume. Because of the expeditious reporting, more and more requests were being generated for different types of analyses. The productive *feedback* cycle was in full operation.

The Data Processing management woke up! They began seeing reports that people were using that they had not knowingly generated. They also noted a sharp increase in usage from the remote facility. The R&D and product development centers started requesting more disk space on the mainframe. These activities were slowing down the standard mainframe processing cycle because of the heavy usage of complex statistics and other applications.

This is the ultimate in guerrilla warfare! Several of the departments, with R&D leading the charge, were using the data communications interface with the mainframe for their own processing. Data processing expected that the interfaces would be used for inquiry only. The data processing department was exposed. They were serving their own interests and not those of the corporation. They fell asleep in their own arrogant elitism. He who snoozes, loses!

Needless to say, a lot of political hell broke loose. It was too late. Productivity finally won out over politics. As Commander Grace Murray Hopper of the U. S. Navy said: *"Don't ask for permission. Go ahead and do it. You can always apologize later if it doesn't work."*

Subsequent to these events, the data processing group attempted to do all the contract administration, project development and implementation. They managed to deliver an early network of PC's that failed miserably. They knew that they should cooperate, but still failed to communicate with and listen carefully to the functional end user departments.

Another round of guerrilla warfare was beginning to form. The end users began looking for a way to connect with each other using an alternative mainframe. Some groups contracted with outside time-sharing organizations. Again, this was something else they could hide in their budgets.

The data processing department activities were saved from being discovered by top management because the company was acquired by another organization. Top management was too busy polishing the outside of the apple to find the worms inside of it!

The politics of the acquisition and the bottom line orientation also destroyed organizational R&D. In a corporate merger, the MBA types seldom consider things like R&D. To them, it is just an unnecessary expense. This is just another example of the unfortunate scenario that has destroyed many businesses in America during the 1970's and 1980's and opened the door to foreign competition.

The very creative development and experimentation that occurred at this rural "skunkworks" was incredible. It could never have been accomplished had this Research Center been convenient to the Headquarter's location.

It has been proven over and over again that real inventiveness, innovation, creativity, and implementations occur in small groups that are removed from the view of the standard corporate bureaucracy. The Manhattan Project, the first operational jet fighter, APPLE Computer, The Poloroid Camera, Digital Equipment Corporations' PDP 11 computer, The SR-71 "BlackBird," the Sidewinder Missle, the CRAY supercomputer, are a few examples that deserve mention.

> *"The skunkworks is not just the most productive show in town, it is the only way complex problems get solved. Every alternative to the skunkworks is known to fail.... Errors must be made. Learning must take place. Feedback must flourish."*
>
> William L. Livingston

CHAPTER 19

THE LONG RANGE PLAN

This is an actual Long Range Planning Approach for a Client Services organization that had just spent over five million dollars. The spoils were shared by a major computer vendor interested only in selling hardware, and a consulting organization that did not develop or define an integrated planning process and implementation scheme.

The VP of client services had abandoned his responsibility. He was totally ignorant about the technical nature of the projects. He also did not realize that all he needed was to apply good management techniques and proper use of competent outside resources.

The major purpose of this variant of the LRP was to get the client to focus on resolving present situations first!

To: Long Range Planning Committee

From: John Benton

The purpose of this document is the presentation of a methodology to define the present environment of your clients in the use of computer applications and develop a needs analysis for expansion of your services to clients for the next five years. In order to implement a strategic plan, *you must stabilize and provide quality service to clients with the present applications.* Then, the long range plan may be implemented to provide expanded growth through new and enhanced services to your clients.

This Document is divided into the following major sections:

Section I. **Customer Environment**
(Strategic)

Section II. **Data Center Environment**
(Strategic)

Section III. **Software Analysis**
(Strategic)

Section IV. **Hardware Selection**
(Tactical)

Section V. **Author Summary and Concerns**

The following is a general outline/checklist document that should be used with *each* service or product. Each application document should feed into this *master* outline so that a summary of combined needs and scheduling can be properly executed.

I. Customer/Client Environment

A. Hardware used for data I/O
   1. Microcomputer(s)
   2. "Dumb" terminals
   3. Manual Submission (paper)
   4. Mass transactions (batch -tape/disk(ette))
      a) mail
      b) data communications

B. Customer/Client standards and procedures (Manuals)
   1. Data formats
   2. Processing Environment
   3. Organizational Considerations
   4. How requirements analyzed and communicated
   5. Industry Regulations and Professionalism

C. End user node demographics
   1. Geography of nodes
      a) Transactions per node *
         (High—Average—Low) I/O.
      b) Number of nodes
   2. Security Considerations
   3. Transaction accounting/audit trail/status
   4. Support Responsibility
      a) Client—Internal Support
      b) Center—Support for Client Leader (C.4.a)
      c) Training—node users (Center+Client)

D. Data Communications Analysis
   1. Hardware—modems, line concentrators, FEP, etc.
   2. Protocols
   3. VAN Services—Telenet, Timenet, etc.
   4. Client Internal Services
   5. Present Volumes
   6. Future Volumes

D. Data Communications Analysis (Continued)
   7. Standards—VAN, LAN, Time-Sharing
   8. Interface with Common Carriers (AT&T, BOC's,)

      * Need common definition of transaction, node, equipment, etc.

II. Data Center Environment (I/O)

A. Data Communications
   1. Volumes—Number of transactions (I/O)
   2. Inquiry—Interactive and Batch
   3. Update—Interactive and Batch
   4. Protocols
   5. Hardware
      a) multiprocessor - FEP
      b) direct to mainframe
   6. Number of concurrent users (interactive)
      a) average
      b) peak
      c) batch processing impacts
   7. Transaction data structuring
      a) Input to processing programs
      b) Output from processing programs

III. Processing Software Analysis

A. Present
   1. Data file record structures
      a) Input Transaction records
      b) History Files
      c) Processing Files (Static and Interim)
      d) Output Transaction Records
   2. Data file volumes
      a) Input Transaction records

b) History Files
c) Processing Files (Static and Interim)
d) Output Transaction Records
e) Archives
f) Maintenance Requirements (Test Files)

3. Operations
   a) Maintenance
   b) Backups
   c) Security
   d) Standards and Procedures
4. Programs
   a) What Works?
   b) What doesn't work? Why?
5. Data Communications
   a) Protocols
   b) VAN Services Telenet, Timenet, etc.
   c) Interface with Common Carriers (AT&T, BOC's,)
   d) Volumes—Number of (I/O) transactions
   e). Number of concurrent users (interactive)

B. Future
   1. Determine Present Data File Requirements (From III.A.1. and III.A.2.)
   2. Determine Present Transaction Requirements (From II.A.)
   3. Validate Present Program(s) Status (From III.A.4.)
   4. Interviews and Surveys
      a) Corporate Facility
      b) Large Client Companies
   5. Outside Sources
      a) Industry Statistics
      b) Competitive Statistics
      c) Government Statistics

6. Determine Rate of Growth (From III.B.4 and III.B.5)
   a) Interactive Transactions
   b) Batch Transactions
   c) Data File Requirements
7. Consolidate Requirements Forecast (From III.B.4 through III.B.6)

III. C. Future Considerations

1. Expansion of Data Bases
   a) Record Formats
   b) Size (Number of Records)
2. New Services to Clients
   a) Develop
   b) Purchase
3. Maintenance Considerations
   a) Data Bases
   b) Application Programs
   c) Systems Software (OS)
4. Accounting
   a) Automated Billing
   b) Successful/Unsuccessful Searches, Lost Info, etc.
5. Auditing
   a) Transaction Tracing, Data Center and Data Comm.
   b) User Information and Statistics
6. Formulate Test (prototype) Models

IV. Hardware Selection & Implementation

A. Use information from Section III—
   Processing Software Analysis
   (III.B.7.—Consolidate Requirements Forecast
   and III.C.)

B. Software
   1. Selection/Development/Conversion
      a) Determine Future Data Base Structures
      b) Finalize future communications—
         growth/protocols
      c) Select programs/methodologies
         for redesigned data base(s)—including simple
         updates, indexing and report generation
         capability (inquiry & standard) Built in
         status/accounting.
      d) Automatic features—all software—
         Checkpoint, restart, backup, error audit trails,
         user help facilities, utilities, sorts, etc.
      e) Implementation alternatives— Corporate,
         Offload to Customer site, VAN, Common
         Carriers, Time-Sharing Companies.

C. Possible Choices Depend on:
   1. Data Communications Transaction Volumes
      a) Interactive
      b) Batch
   2. Data Center Processing Volumes
      a) Data Files
      b) C.P.U.—Internal computer Speed.
   3. Data Structures—
      a) I/O (all)
      b) DASD

4. File Processing—DBMS and Operating System
   a) DBMS Relational, Hierarchal, Network, Combination
   b) OS to handle above choice
5. Controls on Use of outside services
   a) VAN
   b) Common Carrier
   c) Time-Sharing
   d) Service Bureau
   e) Consultants

D. Hardware Install/Test
1. Software Testing
   a) Model(s) testing
   b) Initial Installation and Customer Beta Test
   c) Growth to full client services

E. Upgrade Path
1. Central Control through FEP— Mainframe
2. Distributed Computing
   a) Regional Facilities
   b) Customer Systems Support— Facilities Mgt.
3. Use of Outside Services
   a) Time-Sharing
   b) Common Carrier
   c) VAN

V. Author Summary and Concerns

During the analysis/development cycle for a new system, we are really seeking to perform a design task that accomplishes the following:

1. Make tasks as simple as possible,
2. Take future probable changes into account, and
3. Accept user variation with minimum disturbance to the system.

Some Suggestions:

COMMON LANGUAGE—we should build a list of terms so that all parties and client companies all speak the same language. Here are some examples: claim, loss, transaction, protocol, interactive, node, batch static file, interim file, record, security (node, data center, data transmission, outside services, consultants), backup test model, automatic features, accounting, audit, upgrade, etc.

There should be an increase in frequent, but short teleconferencing to maintain person to person communication and resolve issues.

Strict control of any changes to systems, applications, or data files must be implemented with a documentation trail. Procedure and documentation manuals implementation will accomplish this.

Document and review (walk–throughs) of all program, data base or system flow changes. This information helps in transition to future systems.

The boundaries between humans and automated parts of the system must be carefully monitored, both from a technical and political standpoint.

SUMMARY OF IMPLEMENTATION SCHEDULE

Section I—**Client Environment**

Section II—**Data Center Environment**

Section III—**Processing Software Analysis**

A. Present

B. Future
Validate Present Programs
Interviews/Surveys
Determine Rate of Growth
Consolidation Forecast
Software Selection

Section IV—**Hardware Implementation**

A. Facilities Preparation

B. Financial Coordination

C. Scheduling Commitments

ISSUES TO BE ADDRESSED IN NEAR FUTURE

Definition of Training and Development:

Training is tactical. This is training at the sales office level, operations training in the data center(s), hot line management, etc. Training is the equipping of personnel with capabilities to handle the day to day operations and information flow.

Development is strategic. This is the education of leadership in the client locations and at the center. A clear picture of the corporate and client objectives and the steps to accomplish those objectives must be kept in focus.

The objectives of training and development are most prominent in Section III.B.4, 6, and 7.

FUTURE ACTION TO BE TAKEN

The Long Range Planning group should get together soon to review this document and rearrange activities. A suggested approach is to pick an average client and fill in the details of the above LRP outline. *This will generate necessary, immediate feedback so that this approach can be enhanced and successfully implemented across the client base.*

Any Questions?

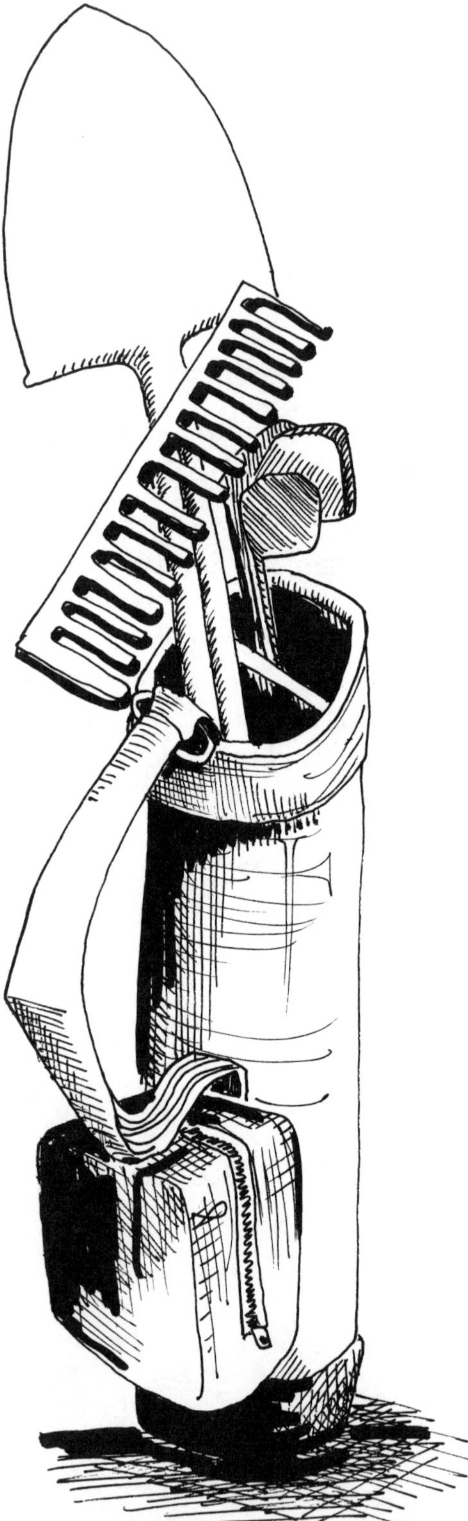

CHAPTER 20

VENDOR MARKETING STRATEGY

(The following, slightly modified, was published in the May 1982 issue of "Software Digest," under the title, "Ecology of Software.")

The relationship between software and the software development environment is crucial for the full understanding of issues in software technology. We need to discuss some of the competitive industry environment and marketing relationships, in relation to the forces shaping the struggle to centralize control of decentralized minicomputer and microcomputer purchases.

From the perspective of the Independent Consultant, there is a clear pattern in the current efforts of data processing departments to regain control over minicomputer and microcomputer procurement in their organizations.

The history of the purchasing behavior of corporations contributes to the *"old"* selling behavior of the computer hardware vendor. The central control issues of data processing departments have been totally changed by the historical and technological changes of the computer industry. Before the late 1960s, the data processing departments were technically separate entities serving the business needs of corporations. In the late 1960s and 1970s, the computer became a commodity item in a consumer marketplace. The rules changed.

Another cause of this *"old"* pattern is the hardware vendor's equipment selling cycle, and the impact of this selling strategy on the user organization's information systems services. The selling organizations hung on to their old strategies and continue to do so.

> *"If you stay in the brine long enough, you become a pickle."* Prescott's Pickle Principle. (Courtesy of Gerry Weinberg.)

The software bottleneck, originating from the very highly structured mainframe computer environment, generated the decentralized procurement of minicomputers and personal computers within the organization. The end users, with their own budgets, began to solve their own departmental problems, independent of the central data processing structure. Computers became affordable and consultants became available.

Here is how the computer vendor account management strategy works. The computer hardware vendor is in the business of selling *equipment*. The representatives are usually well educated and well informed about their product line, and can do excellent studies on their customers requirements. They are also expert at orienting those needs toward the hardware they would most like to sell. Vendors like to sell to a large *central* location, that is, one location. They cultivate an inside champion over whom they have complete control. The *goal* of the hardware vendor is to exercise control of data processing decisions within the customer account so that the vendor can profit greatly.

The proper administration of data processing within the account is of *secondary* interest to the vendor. The vendor is always very, very sure that the *responsibility* lies *entirely* with the customer management. The vendor makes a lot of decisions regarding various activities for which the customer has ultimate responsibility. You can be sure that the customer data processing management takes the lumps when things do not work out. All kinds of comments are made by the vendor during the selling process. The customer is *led to believe* that the vendor's recommendation for the implementation of a large centrally controlled facility will serve all the people in the organization. The vendor's verbal claims will seldom be seen in writing.

The installation of the hardware is usually months, if not years, away. The vendor sales/management team that sold to the facility is almost always different from the installation team. This results in an applications backlog. When the vendor has the customer commitment for a large central facility in the future, activities within the account for needed computer capacity are frozen. This means that there is virtually no development activity. This also makes the vendor's life easier by keeping competitive vendors out of the account.

It is *exactly* at this point that some interim plans should be implemented so that eventual transition to the large central facility is smoother. Vendor control of these data processing decisions results in end users suffering and being buried under their own paper work for many months until the central facility is *scheduled* to help them. They rapidly outgrow the available computer resources needed to expedite their departmental functions.

When the system(s) is delivered, the main data processing functions usually improve, often through myriad installation problems, and *some* of the more important ancillary programs for the non-data processing end users may get implemented. For the most part, however, the people in the trenches do not get their non-scheduled processing requirements met.

So there are the great promises, usually implied and undocumented from the vendor and parrotted by the data processing personnel, that do not come to fruition. There has been little application growth by the user departments. Nothing has been developed for many months, and the inefficiencies of the company's operations suddenly become very apparent. Now the promises are delayed even further! The computer aided management functions and requirements for the planning in a dynamic company are now *lost* in an atmosphere of anger and distrust.

The next occurrences are the decentralized acquisition of small computers. The conflict accelerates. The end user departments need money for additional personnel, equipment and outside services to solve their problems. The corporate management will not allocate more dollars. *Justifiably,* the President or Executive Vice President says: "Look at all the money that has been spent for computer hardware, make it work." Now the data processing manager takes his lumps for putting himself totally in the hands of his "trusted" computer hardware vendor. The end users continue their burial rites under paper. Remember, the end users had a year or two head start with inefficient operations! Eventually, the department managers hide a minicomputer or microcomputers in their budget expenditures so that they can get their work done at the department level. The corporate officers look the other direction. As the company continues to grow, the central facility becomes loaded with more data on standard applications.

> *"Romer's Rule says that the biggest and longest lasting changes usually originate in attempts to preserve the very thing that ultimately changes most."*
>
> Gerry Weinberg

It doesn't take a nuclear physicist to see that most functional end user computing again occurs outside of the central data processing department.

Here is how the computer hardware vendor again implements the adaptive account management strategy. Once again, the cycle is compete. It started with vendor control. The hardware was installed. The vendor got his money. The customer has severe political problems between the data processing department and the users. The users acquire and use minicomputers, personal computers, independent consultants and outside services. Standard applications fill the central facility. More computing resources are needed, both at the centralized and decentralized levels. The vendor arrives on the scene and will magically collect this great morass into one centrally controlled facility. History again attempts to repeat itself. Now the cycle is complete. It started with vendor control. The hardware was installed. The vendor got his money.....

The vendor now has a "full line" of minicomputer and microcomputer products and services and will "link up" with the centralized facility, providing a "distributed" system over a "network." Once again, all kinds of comments are made during the selling process. Once again, the customer is *led to believe* that the vendor's recommendations for the implementation of a large distributed system will serve all the people within the organization. Once again, the cycle is complete. History again attempts to repeat itself, *and tragically, does*. It starts with vendor control..

CHAPTER 21

THE PHYSICIAN'S OFFICE

The following was assembled with the assistance of Ms. Cindy DeBerg, Professor and Chair, Medical Records Technology, at Oakton Community College in Des Plaines, Illinois.

This is a categorized outline of identifiable problems regarding the collection of fees and related activities for medical services provided by a medical office practice management service organization. This is a necessary document so that the services can be marketed appropriately and responsibilities assigned.

The physicians need clear, concise documentation so that they fully understand the responsibilities of their service provider, their office activities and their professional financial responsibilities. In general, physicians have a difficult time relating to anything that is not "medical." Worse yet, most have no idea about the actual financial position of their practices.

The Categories:

I. The Office Staff Clerical Functions

II. Physician Responsibilities

III. Hospital Responsibilities

IV. Patient Responsibilities

V. Regulatory Concerns

I. The Office Staff Clerical Functions

1. Paper Involvements as a Result of Patient Engagement
    a. Check Coding for Diagnoses/Treatment
    b. Appropriate Level of Service?
    c. Critical Care Codes
    d. Appropriate Sequence Listing of Surgical Procedures
    e. Using Coding Modifiers Correctly
    f. Appropriate Medical Terminology
    g. Feedback to Physician on What is Allowable
    h. Feedback to Physician on Changes in Regulations
    i. Patient Aware of What is Covered
    j. Superbill Changes and Design
    k. Handling of Non-Approved Medicare Diagnosis
    l. Receivables Management:
        i. Monitoring of Third Party Payment
        ii. EOB Monitoring
        iii. Timely Billing/Payment Checking
        iv. Appeal Process Issues
        v. Re-insurance (ex. f. iv.)
    m. HMO Activities
        i. Encounter Forms

ii. Referral Forms
iii. Cancellation List
iv. Stop Loss/Catastrophic Billing

n. Carrier Monitoring
i. Variance in Carrier Practices
What is Paid Denial Pattern Payment Cycle
ii. Variance of Global concept time period for Medicare Advisement
All Pre-surgery Fees Included All Critical Care Documentation Complete
iii. Appeal Process Handling Prevention Response on Denials
iv. HMO Coordination of Benefits with other Insurance Carriers
v. Multiple Price Schedules Control, Review, Revision—Differences in Carrier Services

2. Checking of Patient Demographics (Profile Management)
   a. Insurance Information
   b. Address Information (Home/Company)
   c. Primary/Secondary Coverages
   d. Type of Coverage (Commercial, HMO, etc.)

3. Keeping Track of Dr. Offsite Activities
   a. Hospital Op Reports
   b. Hospital Op Reports Assists
   c. Hospital Visits
   d. "Occasional"—ex. Non-Scheduled Hospital Visits
   e. Emergencies
   f. After Hour and Weekend Activities
   g. Dr. Transcription Legibility - (Verbal and Written)

4. Schedule Management
    a. Patient Appointments
    b. Patient Service at Office (Wait Time?)
    c. Dr. Schedule (Office, Hospital, Emergencies, etc.)

II. Physician Responsibilities

1. Hospital Paper Work to Office—Op Reports

2. "Occasional"—(ex. Non-Scheduled Hospital Visits)

3. Hospital Visits (Scheduled)

4. Emergencies—Inform Office

5. Dr. Transcription Legibility (Verbal and Written)
    a. Accurate
    b. Timely

6. Respond to Office Requests Promptly
    a. So, Doctor, What did you do this weekend?

7. Concurrent Care Issues with other Physicians in Practice

8. Offsite Charges—Surgical Assists, Op Reports, etc.

9. Critical Care Documentation
    a. Cover Letters for Unusual Situations for Carrier
    b. Inform Medicare Patients ahead of time on coverage (Acknowledgment Signature Required)

10. Handling of non-approved Medicare Diagnosis

III. Hospital Responsibilities

1. Expeditious Pursuit and Distribution of Op Reports and Paper Work in General
   a. Primary Physician
   b. Assisting Physician c. Physicians' Offices

2. Medical Records Efficiency
   a. Interrogation and Verification
   b. Competence
   c. Training of Personnel
   d. Coordination with Billing Services/Dr. Offices
   e. Feedback and Follow up between Hospital Departments.

3. Concurrent Care Issues with Physicians' Office(s)

4. Outpatient Logging.

IV. Patient Responsibilities

1. Patient Responsible for:
   a. Payment
   b. Insurance Submission

2. Demographics
   a. Correct Insurance Information
   b. Primary/Secondary
   c. Correct Employment Information
   d. Correct Residential Information

3. Keep Physician Informed
   a. Patient should communicate
   b. Physician should be sure patient communicates

4. Patient should ask what is covered

V. Regulatory Concerns

1. Appropriate Office Personnel to Attend Meetings Sponsored by Carriers.

2. Input From Other Sources
   a. Educational Institutions
   b. Service Organizations
   c. Vendors of Computerized Services
   d. Associations (IMRA, AMRA, etc.)
   e. Literature
   f. Physicians (AMA)

Commentary

The Clerical Administrator at a Medical Office Practice *must be constant guardian at the doorway of information.* He or she must be sure the *information is gathered* as rapidly as possible, *checked* for accuracy and completeness, *entered* into the billing cycle expeditiously, and *followed-up* with tenacity.

This requires pressing the physicians for information, following up with the hospital where necessary, finding the best way to get response from the carriers, and being aware of regulations and technical issues (coding). Above all, it means giving the patient the service deserved at the appropriate billing level.

Although it is the primary responsibility of the Administrator to handle the "office," physicians must do all they can to assist. This not only increases revenues but eliminates a lot of confusion and time wasted in unnecessary follow up.

Yes, the physician's primary mission, purpose, and source of self fulfillment is the practice of medicine. *But, if the physician does not respond to administrative requirements, particularly in the arena of increasing regulation, proper submission of accurate documentation, etc., he or she may find that the resulting financial and legal liabilities cause the loss of the source of psychic and material income.*

V. SOME OTHER TOPICS

Leaders must have the courage to demand excellence, fight ignorance and resolve conflicts.

CHAPTER 22

(The following article was published in the June/July 1988 issue of BUILDER/ARCHITECT Magazine.)

SO, YOU WANT TO BUY A COMPUTER!

We have just what you need. We have just imported the WOMBAT 64 parallel processor from Australia. It is easy to use, costs less than any other personal computer, and it is compatible with everything, including your microwave oven and the dishwasher!

This 64 bit, 33 megahertz machine sports 8 megabytes of RAM, high density multi-megabyte diskettes of various sizes and densities, an 80 megabyte hard disk, a high raster density VGA color board and monitor, and the options for many more peripheral devices such as plotters, barcode readers, optical jukeboxes with skuzzy(SCUSI) worm drives, modems and your garage door opener.

Did you get all that?

Well yes, you say, the part about the microwave oven, dishwasher and garage door opener—then you lost me!

Wait a minute, Did I say *"Personal Computer."* There are about eight definitions of the word *"personal"* in Webster's Dictionary. The one most closely related to computers is, *"concerning a particular individual's intimate affairs, interests or activities."*

How intimate do you want to be with your computer?

Do you really want to have an affair with one? It could break your heart.

Is the only thing personal about personal computers the fact that you write a personal check to purchase one?

Is *"personal computer"* actually an oxymoron? You all know what an oxymoron or apparent contradiction in terms is, don't you? (Expressions like: military intelligence, plastic glasses, congressional oversight, men working, country music, etc.).

Putting cynicism aside, what are the myths and realities of obtaining and using a personal computer? First of all, if you can live without a computer, maybe you don't need one. Do you want a computer for a special purpose or just to impress someone? If you have a disorganized manual system, you will have a poorer computer system. Just think, with a computer, mistakes can be made thousands of times faster!

Lets look at the Myths!

Myth #1 - Ease of Use

This is a relative term. If you have used computers in the past, then ease of use is meaningful. For the experienced computer user, yes, computers are easier to use. It is easier to make the transition to a different computer or software application. There are many more ready-made applications that make them easier to use than in the past. However, if you have *never* used a computer, ease of use is *absolutely meaningless*. If you are a user with limited experience, there are many traps awaiting you.

For instance, if you look at a computer keyboard, you will see some familiar keys; the numbers across the top and the alphabetic layout similar to a typewriter. But what are F1, F2, F3, . . . F12, esc, ctrl, alt, pause, break, scroll lock, SysRq, ins, del, home, end, and all the keys with the funny arrows and symbols? When and how are these special keys used? Just the keyboard is enough to *fully panic* novices, particularly if they are unfamiliar with the basic typewriter keyboard. Other areas such as the use of a laser printer with all the different fonts, different sizes and densities of diskettes, choices for hard drives, the mouse, etc. are all difficult for the novices as well as users with limited experience.

> *Ease of use is an individual definition. Ease of use changes as more training and experience is gained!* This leads us to —

Myth #2 - Inexpensive

If you measure expense just in terms of what a computer costs and the potential of what it can do, this is a valid premise. But, how much must *you* do to get it working? How much of *your* own time, or *your* employees time can you afford to get the applications on the computer functional? How much is *your* time worth. Is there a deadline that depends on the use of the computer. What are the costs of missing it? Will *you* get roped into *"buying now and coping later?"*

Peter Drucker says that action without thinking is the cause of every failure! There are a lot of computers with permanent potential. Permanent potential means that there is a device or a person that is capable of performing all kinds of tasks, but the tasks are *never* completed, or perhaps not even started, but the potential is there!

Potential is *useless* until it becomes kinetic, or put into motion. The cost of the computer is not just the purchase price!

What are the training costs? What does special purpose programming cost? Are there maintenance considerations? Where are you going to put it? Environment?

The computer itself supplies *only* the potential for doing something. *It takes people and time to get things done!*

Here are some other considerations:

Where is the computer going to be placed in the office? What about the human factors? Lighting? Noise levels? Ergonomics?

What is the value received as a result of a successful installation? Cost savings? More available decision making information? Replacement of personnel? (This is usually a fallacy, particularly in a small business.) Time Savings? Scheduling?

Computer vendors measure expense to you in how much money is made from the hardware and software. In other words, their income! Therefore, the more computer vendors can use the myth of *inexpensive,* the more advantageous it is to them. *How do you measure expense!*

Myth #3 - Compatibility

Computers are more compatible than they ever have been. As a matter of fact, they are so compatible that it is more difficult to identify some of the incompatibilities! When someone says a computer or computer application is compatible, be from

Missouri and say *"show me."* Better yet, a good question to ask is: *"If the computer and software do not work as you claim, will you take it back and refund the purchase price and related cost of trying to use it?"* The assumption of compatibility has been the downfall of many!

An example of the compatibility issue is the various data densities on diskettes that look the same. A given diskette, by physical appearance may hold approximately 100 pages of single spaced typewritten information or 350 pages of typewritten information. Can you tell which is which just from looking at the diskette? If a computer has a disk reader for the lower density, that is, the 100 page diskette, but you have the higher density media, that is, the 350 page diskette, you have a problem. Classically, it is the problem of stuffing 35 pounds of chicken fat in a 10 pound bag! Someone told you it was compatible, not realizing he has a higher density diskette reader than you have.

How can you avoid being trapped by these myths?

First of all, before you even look at a computer, write down what you want from it. Do you want it for: educational purposes; a combination of education and home business computing; or, straight business computing applications such as accounting, construction cost tracking and reporting, forms design, graphics, architectural drawings, engineering drawings, word processing, project management, general information retrieval for departmental management, industrial engineering, data collection, etc.

A computer manufacturer or salesmen is not needed to tell you what you want from the computer!

You can do many of the functions to determine your needs.

You can determine the reporting requirements, and probably most of the steps for deciding the data input requirements and required processing methodologies such as word processing, budgets or data inquiry. Do as much as you and your employees can do before calling for help. *Then find a competent, independent, knowledgeable source for outside intervention, before you contact a computer retailer.*

This may look like an extra expense at first, but planning will save you a lot of confusion, time, grief and probably money later on. If you are looking for adventure, don't plan.

> *"Adventure is the result of poor planning."*
> Colonel Blatchford Snell

Brian Tracy said: *"Every minute spent in planning... spent in thinking about the job, saves 10 to 12 minutes in execution."*

Don't spend a lot of time looking for "deals." The few dollars saved from a mail order house or discount software vendor may turn into many time consuming and therefore, costly, problems.

The real costs in obtaining a computer are in the training of personnel and development and/or installation of the applications on the computer. *You get what you pay for!*

Remember, *Prior Planning Prevents Poor Performance!*

CHAPTER 23

(The following article was generated during studies at an IBM Systems Research Institute and published in the May 1977 issue of SMALL BUSINESS COMPUTOR. The sexist nature of the original text has been modified, but the content is 1967 vintage.)

1990 in 1967?

(AN EXERCISE IN IMAGINATION)

This essay describes future applications with what is, at present, technologically feasible. A major area of future application will be the use of time-sharing computer terminals within a virtual data base in all homes. These terminals will feature voice recognition and visual display (CRT) type operations.

The data base will include such areas as the public library, weather bureau, bus and airline schedules, train schedules, price lists from all major companies, recipes, formulas, auto routes and distances, etc. Each major company or organization will have a data base that may be interrogated with the use of voice recognition. A computer at a local message switching center will direct the inquiry over communications lines to the applicable data base, or, direct contacts can be made by the home if the required data base location is known.

The terminal will also make available to the home facilities for writing programs to solve mathematical, physical, engineering or other applicable problems. This includes children's homework and the business problems the adults bring home. In fact, the adults will be able to interrogate their company's data base just as if they were at the office. If they forget a report and want to review some part of the operation, it will be possible to get the data by using the home terminal. Of course, there will be file security to prevent unauthorized use of personal, and confidential, documents not applicable to the area of endeavor.

Orders can be placed for the week's groceries, but not until after the terminal had worked out the week's menu, scanned the local markets for the best prices and run this all through a optimizing program to determine the best buy by using factors such as cost to drive to the different markets, which would waste time and money. In fact, when approved, the order will take place automatically, allowing it to be picked up immediately.

All outstanding bills could be interrogated and checked against the budget. The terminal helped work this out at the beginning of the month or year. You would be notified when you overspent in any particular area and corrective measures would be suggested. (Hot dogs next week instead of steak, and lay off the booze!)

At the end of the year it will prepare your taxes for you, and ask you to supply any missing information so that good ol' Uncle Sam can be remunerated.

The combination of a virtual data base with a time-sharing computer terminal in the home will give the average family more computer power than exists today in our largest installations.

To obtain this, two factors are necessary.

1. *An inexpensive terminal*
2. *Unlimited communication facilities such as helical waveguides and lasers.*

These capabilities will certainly come to pass in the next 20 years.

Although there are problems with a gigantic data base and file security, this type of at-home information retrieval and processing is certainly feasible. This establishes a need for both more voice grade transmission as well as high speed transmission of huge amounts of data from computer to computer. The huge data base and volume of transmission unquestionably creates a need for a huge amount of computational equipment.

The population growth of the world and resource allocation to service and develop the cultures of the world will require fantastic communications capability. Some examples are the reception and routing of messages, permanent and intermediate storage of large amounts of data, subsequent retrieval and display of information from and for the housewife to the national leaders to people on the moon for information on everything from recipes to retro-fire.

The impact on IBM and the rest of the computing field by the year 2000 is an expansion of 100 times what it is today. The speed and volume at which data is processed will make the System 360 an object of curiosity and wonder in the museums of the future.

CHAPTER 24

THE FALLACY OF COMPATIBILITY AND THE CORPORATE DATA BASE

Those of us that have been in the computer arena for many years have constantly heard the word *"compatibility,"* probably one of the most overused and misused words in the computer industry. With the advent of inexpensive mass data storage, we are now hearing the phrase *"universal data base."* The alleged reason for the universal data base is so that everyone in a corporation is using the same numbers to do their work. This is valid in concept only.

The truth of the matter is that few of these universal data bases will ever become a reality. Why? There are three principal reasons.

First, departmental data dynamics may change too rapidly for the corporate data base to keep up, both in content and user access. For example, how quickly does marketing find out about engineering changes?

Second, the talent may not exist in most corporations to maintain the data base, modify accessing mechanisms and update reporting programs for the breadth of end users who are not computer professionals. In other words, the predictability in size and use of the data base is suspect.

The *third* and most important reason is that there are many conflicting methodologies and environments relative to computer use in the organization. For instance, the access mechanisms and data volume requirements are quite different for engineering drawings versus accounting records.

The corporate data base concept is valid for those segments of an organization where there is little structural change to the data files and programs. This environment has many known qualities. The schedule for computer usage is fixed (the payroll is run every Wednesday). The file sizes and structures are fixed. The personnel are knowledgeable. However, the extension and use of this knowledge across all functional activities of a corporation is suspect.

The central role of data processing is to maintain *historical* data on as current a basis as possible. The role of the end user departments, such as Research & Development, marketing, engineering, special products and services, etc. are looking to the *future* and examining "what if?" phenomena. Computer usage in this environment is non-scheduled, time dependent ("We gotta do it now!"), and unpredictable in required data and content.

When these differences are unrecognized, a technical and political conflict erupts because of the *centralized corporate resource trap*. It becomes very difficult for the functional departments in large corporations to get their work done because of this myth of the corporate data base. The end users and data processing people must patiently educate one another so that proper use of computing resources can occur. What should be centralized? What should be distributed? What should stand alone and be independent?

The added benefit of recognizing conflicting requirements is that when processing methodologies and data requirements are defined outside of the *"universal data base"* and main processing environment, movement of data and/or programs is more expeditious. Environments are clearly defined within functional or departmental areas. Therefore, there is greater understanding when explanation or transfer of information is required by another functional area. There is less conflict, more productive discussion and cooperation because each group has control over its functional activities. The functional groups also develop an understanding of computer requirements. They become more computer literate. This helps when their applications move to, or interface with, the corporate mainframe.

Feedback, information interchange, mutual respect and cross training of various groups will make the computers follow the corporate long-range plan. When too much centralization of data occurs, bureaucratic empires evolve and strangle the corporation.

Has the phrase *"universal data base"* upstaged the word *"compatibility"* in the arena of misuse and abuse?

CHAPTER 25

(Author Note: Resources for much of the following material are from audio tapes and literature from Nightingale-Conant)

PROFESSIONALISM - WHAT IS IT?

More than Education,

More than Experience,

More than Training,

It's a State of Mind,

A Combination of Skill and Dedication.

We all know a professional when we see one. Do we know what makes the individual a professional? Is it the organization he or she is associated with? Is it because the individual is a doctor, lawyer, CPA, policeman, or car salesman? There are professionals in all these categories, and unfortunately some who are not professional.

Is professionalism the work a person does, or how the individual performs the work? Some action words we get from the dictionary definition of a professional are: devotion, ethics, standards, engaging, pursue, livelihood, satisfaction, and a word many find offensive, conform. Conform, in this context, is very proper, because it means conforming to *ethical, moral* and, therefore, *professional* standards. The professional is engaged, intensely involved and committed in his or her activities.

We hear about "acting" or "being" professional. For instance, how many times have we heard or said: "Be sure you call in advance for appointments." "Be on time." "Follow up with phone calls and literature." "Be sensitive to people and surroundings." We have heard them all many times, but are we consistently doing these things?

If we do not deliberately form good habits, then unconsciously, we will form bad ones! Call your clients or customers when things are going well! Show them you are interested. Don't wait for them to call with a problem!

You see, professionalism does not just happen. It is a result of carefully nurtured and fully developed habits. Again, these habits make a difference. The next step is to link these *habits* with a *definite purpose.*

The mark of a true professional is a person that is always productive or attempting to produce, no matter what the external circumstances. Our future does not depend totally on economic conditions, outside influences or circumstances beyond our control. Our future depends on practical purpose (not fantasy), infused with desire.

How do you feel inside when you have had several days or weeks of no progress. We cannot always help how we feel, and we should not feel guilty if we feel a little low once in a while. Sam Lilly of the National Speakers Association wrote: *"If you want to stop along the road and lick your professional wounds, that is OK. Just be careful you do not become a professional licker, rather than a professional speaker."* All professionals have times when they feel depressed, but you will never see them act depressed. They are enthusiastic, for they know that enthusiasm is the mainspring of success.

Did you know that successful professionals have formed the habit of doing things that failures do not like to do? If you were to make a functional list of your work activities and evaluate them, you would have at least one thing you do not like to do. I know that in my consulting work, my least favorite task is documentation. But I enjoy the rest of my work so much that I perform this necessary function. If I were to let it go, I would lose a lot of my effectiveness!

After doing this kind of evaluation, ask yourself:

1. *Is there an overlap of what I am doing now and what I would like to do?*
2. *Is there an overlap of what I am doing now and my long term objective?*
3. *Is there an area I am not doing, do not like, but must do to obtain my objective, which has more positive aspects than negative ones?*

Success involves doing some things you do not like to do to get the self esteem and material things you desire. To further clarify where we want to go, we must ask this final penetrating question:

> *If I keep on doing what I am doing now, will it get me where I want to go?*

Professionals recognize that accomplishment lies in the risk of using their strength and knowledge to assist their peers, rather than the singular goal of pressing for personal advancement at the expense of others. I read a definition of hell a while back. It is in the form of a question.

> *"Is hell a state where everyone is perpetually concerned about his own dignity and advancement, where everyone has a grievance, and where every one lives the deadly serious passions of envy, self-importance, and resentment?"*

This is definitely not the attitude and environment of a professional.

WHAT ARE THE CHARACTERISTICS OF THE SUCCESSFUL PROFESSIONAL?

Successful professionals develop the habit of pressing their limits and making their lives larger. This keeps zest and enthusiasm in their lives. They must overcome many of the habits and prejudices that have made them slaves. Many of these were instilled in them as children.

So, as growing professionals we have:

FIRST: Formation of good habits.

SECOND: Clearly defined and established goals.

Why does the professional survive? Remember, if you are really good, you become a target for all the losers. Were you a really good student in school? Did you separate yourself from the crowd? Did you happen to know the "right people?"

Were you "lucky?" Professionals survive because they know that luck is where preparation, hard work and opportunity meet! The professional believes the Hindu proverb that says: "Nobility is being superior to your previous self." You *all* know what a proverb is. It is a short sentence based on long experience.

The best leaders do not seek positions of leadership, but demonstrate it in their own lives. Professionals love people and use things, not vice versa.

The key element found in most successful professionals is not the fact that they do something new or different, but the fact that they do things better!

The following story about Henry Royce is an expansion based on some materials from the Nightingale-Conant organization.

Henry Royce did not invent the motorcar. He just thought it was too heavy and inefficient. In Manchester, England on April 1, 1904, a beautiful motorcar appeared, with no clatter from the engine, no grinding of gears. This was indeed something to marvel at in an age when the motor car sounded like a repetitive clatter of dishes falling from the cupboard shelves. The trade name of ROLLS-ROYCE went on to become the trade name for anything excellent or outstanding.

Henry Royce and C. S. Rolls did not do anything new. They just made something better. *Finding ways to do things better is the surest path to success.*

Henry Royce was so wrapped up in his work, he would not eat for days at a time. Modern Management Consultant Guru Tom Peters did not invent the management by walking around philosophy. (MBWA). As a matter of fact, MBWA was first done by God when he was looking for Adam and Eve in the

Garden of Eden. Henry Royce took it to the extreme! He would sleep overnight in the factory! They would have a young lad follow him around the factory with milk and a sandwich so that he would eat. He once heard a mechanic say, "That's good enough." They had to hold Henry Royce back. Only excellence was good enough for Henry Royce and his partner C. S. Rolls.

More than 35 years later, British fighter planes, the well known Spitfires, helped turn the tide against Germany in the famed Battle of Britain during the early years of WWII. These aircraft were powered by Rolls-Royce Engines.

One of the stained glass windows in the Rolls-Royce Aircraft engine factory, has this inscription regarding the Spitfire pilots: "Who in the Battle of Britain, turned the work of our hands into the salvation of our country."

The professional demand for excellence, the ripples of commitment and dedication of Henry Royce carried forward for more than three decades. *His professionalism had a hand in saving a nation!*

Being professional is a responsibility we all have, not only to ourselves, but to others. Our actions of the moment can have a far reaching *"ripple"* effect, just like a stone dropped in the water. What kind of ripples are you making?

Professionals think about difficult problems and come up with possible solutions. They don't accept the first solution they find. They know that most solutions are temporary until something better comes along. They recognize that intelligent discussion is more important than pat answers. They soon recognize that everything they know may not be so.

In the play, The King and I, the king laments:

> *"When I was a boy,*
> *World was better spot.*
> *What was so was so, what was not was not.*
> *Now I am a man,*
> *world has changed a lot.*
> *Some things nearly so,*
> *others nearly not.*
> *There are times I think I am not sure of what I absolutely know.*
> *Very often find confusion in conclusion I concluded long ago.*
> *In my head are many facts that as a Student I have studied to procure.*
> *In my head are many facts, of which, I wish I was more certain I was sure."*

He continues with his self examining dialog about his problems as a leader, how to lead his country, how to tell his son to lead and still be honest with himself, and how to handle personal relationships. He is very alone and introspective, as most professionals tend to be from time to time, knowing that he does not live in a fixed world with pat answers. He finishes his reflection:

> *"If the Lord in Heaven do not show the way,*
> *Every day I try to live another day.*
> *If the Lord in Heaven do not show the way,*
> *Every day I do my best for one more day.*
> *But, is a puzzlement!"*

The subject of professionalism appears to be direct and simple in definition at the outset. As you can see, the characteristics of the professional in terms of attitude, involvement, use of logic, possession of desire and direction toward a goal requires a lot of analysis of our external environment and establishment of internal harmony with self.

In closing here are some concluding ideas on the definition of a professional.

Professionals:

- *have standards and stick to them*
- *are enthusiastic about the work*
- *feel good about themselves*
- *are proud of their accomplishments*
- *accept themselves totally and unconditionally*
- *do not devalue themselves through destructive self criticism*
- *have unconditional warm regard for all people at all times.*

The professional is committed!

The professional is like a strong ship, carrying a precious cargo of quality and service, sailing on a wild ocean of mediocrity. This vessel is equipped with a good set of bilge pumps to keep that *sea of procrastination, diversion* and *fear* from swamping it. The bilge pumps have names like *persistence, commitment, direction, love, dedication, tenacity, enthusiasm* and *faith.*

What a great accomplishment when that ship reaches the safety of the tranquil harbor and docks at the pier called goals.

CHAPTER 26

EDUCATIONAL POT POURRI

Although this Chapter is indirectly related to the world of information processing, I feel compelled to make some comments regarding this important aspect of our society. My limited qualifications are that I taught High School Sciences for three years, worked with educational activities in industry, served as a part time professor in Community Colleges, and made sure that we lived in good school districts. There is a very serious side as well as a humorous side to education. The following are some of my *"narrow opinions"* on the subject.

The Educational Environment and Related Creativity

> *"While Japan spends eight times more for education than war, the Arab countries happily spend twenty eight times more on their guns than their textbooks."*
> William L. Livingston

> *"Unfortunately, the 19th century form of education that persists in the USA is a primary example of disjointed, dysfunctional activity, totally unrelated to the real world."*
>
> John T. Benton

But, as with many tragic circumstances, let's take a look at the thoughtful and lighter side...

From a Jesuit School: The Lesson

Then Jesus took his disciples up the mountain and gathering them around him, he taught them, saying...

"Blessed are the Poor in spirit, for theirs is the kingdom of heaven." Then Simon Peter said, "Do we have to write this down?"

"Blessed are the meek." Then Andrew said, "Are we supposed to know this?"

"Blessed are they that mourn." Then James said, "Will we have a test on this?"

"Blessed are the merciful." Then Phillip said, "What if we don't know it?"

"Blessed are they that thirst for justice." Then Bartholomew said, "Do we have to turn this in?"

"Blessed are you when persecuted." Then John said, "The other disciples didn't have to learn this."

"Blessed are you when you suffer." Then Matthew said, "When do we get out of here?"

"Be glad and rejoice for your reward is great in heaven .." Then Judas said, "What does this have to do with real life?"

Then one of the Pharisees present asked to see Jesus' lesson plans and inquired of Jesus his terminal objectives in the cognitive domain ....

JESUS WEPT!

(Source Unknown)

Educational Administration

The teacher's union representative at a negotiation meeting.

"We, the willing, led by the unknowing,
are doing the impossible for the ungrateful.
We have done so much, for so long, with so little,
We are now qualified to do anything with nothing."

Unfortunately, the above statement has more truth than most educators would care to admit.

I taught at the high school level for three years before I renounced the vow of poverty. My primary reason for leaving however was *not* money. Inadequate administrators, a tenure system that encouraged incompetence, and no concept of salary for results achieved were enough motivation for me to seek a more realistic and less dysfunctional environment. The concept of a merit system was and still is, totally foreign to educators.

The problem in education today is *not* money. The problem is clearly the lack of courageous administrators. Too many are afraid of the school board and parents, not to mention their own shadows. When I was teaching, we had a high school principal who was a good disciplinarian. He, and his hand picked guidance counselor, were the only competent administrators in the whole school system. He walked the halls. He intercepted problems early. The parents were called when the problem was beginning to fester, not after the fact. He counseled with his teachers. The classrooms were havens of learning, not battlegrounds.

This school had one of the lowest salary schedules in the area. The school also had the lowest teacher turnover in the area. Teachers from other school districts were calling our principal to be on the list if any positions became available.

Teachers want respect and support more than anything else. I have seen this accomplished. Administrators must have the courage to demand excellence, fight ignorance, and resolve both internal and external conflicts.

In many cases, the parents have no idea or don't care what is happening. The administrators look the other direction as long as they can and the kids are allowed to raise hell. And, the teachers get blamed for poor education.

Sorry, but the teachers are forced to be baby sitters. The only way the teachers have of getting the attention of the administrators, school boards, parents and community is to pursue the salary issues. How can education take place?

Over the years I have done part time teaching at Community Colleges. The Community Colleges are probably going to save education in this country. They can adapt quickly. They have special credit and non-credit courses that are helpful to the people and businesses in the community. They provide the environment for students to catch up and overcome the nearly mortal wounds inflicted on their capabilities by the public school systems.

The standard high school and college curricula need to be addressed in the light of the great social and technological changes in the world. Unfortunately, the desire does not exist within these sedentary, profligate bureaucracies. What will cause the changes? It is already happening. More and more parents are willing to pay the price to send their children to private high schools. There go the votes for increased support for public schools. Colleges are also beginning to go out of business.

All it takes is courage and real leadership to make changes. Is there any out there?

Some Educational Humor

Out of the Mouth of a Child

While in first grade, my daughter asked me why I kept bringing work home from the office every night. I explained that I had so much work to do that I just couldn't finish it during the day. "Then why," she persisted, "don't they put you in a slower group?"

Athletics

I know of one University that has three football squads. One for offense, one for defense, and one to attend classes.

Athletic Directors and Coaches claim that football teaches valuable lessons, such as: For every one person who gives you something, there are eleven who want to take it away.

At a business school, when the quarterback took the ball from the center, he had to sign for it.

Mathematics

Two geometry students were trying to determine the height of a flagpole. A passerby suggested that they lay the flagpole down and measure it. The students replied,"We don't care how long it is, we need to know its height."

Teacher's Problems

My son's teacher quit because of "burnout." I suspect my son is an arsonist.

Our teachers wanted to have power lunches in the faculty lounge. The Board of Education installed a microwave.

Murphy's Laws for Educators

Good students move away.

New students come from schools that don't teach anything.

The teachers' lounge will be the worst room in the school. It will contain dilapidated furniture, one noisy copying machine and coffee cups with penicillin cultures.

The clock in the instructor's room will be wrong.

Students who touch the instructor will have scabies or the bubonic plague.

When speaking to the school psychologist, the teacher will say "weirdo" rather than "emotionally disturbed".

The time taken to explain is inversely proportional to information retained.

The problem child will be the school board member's son.

Clocks will run more quickly during free time.

If the instructor teaches art, the principal will be an ex-coach and will dislike art. If the instructor is a coach, the principal will be an ex-coach who took a winning team to state competition.

A teacher will be ill on a "snow day."

Author Comment: I wonder if Murphy spent six years in high school.

CHAPTER 27

EXECUTIVE INFORMATION DEVELOPMENT GENERAL SYSTEMS WARNING

(The following, slightly modified, was published in the January 1988 issue of "Landscape Contractor.")

The following is a service to our clients in helping them to understand and deal with situations regarding the perversity and unexpected behavior of irrational inanimate objects and suggested appropriate human responses.

Note #1: The nature of any machine.

A machine is more subject to act inappropriately during periods of *Critical Need*. Every machine has a special circuit or device called a *Cybernetic Evaluator (Critical Detector)* that senses the emotional state of the operator in terms of how desperate he or she is to use the machine. This *Human-Machine Interface Detector* then creates a malfunction proportional to the desperation of the operator.

This device knows how to keep a solution to a problem just beyond the reach of the operator. It knows how to keep the operator at just the right level of panic so that logic cannot be used. The *Cybernetic Evaluator* keeps the operator working on the wrong problem for as long a period as possible before it changes to another problem state.

After many hours, the operator may be observed with a blank stare and be unresponsive to simple conversation. Telling the operator to "Have a Nice Day" could be dangerous to your health.

Threatening the machine with violence only aggravates the situation. Likewise, attempts to use another machine may cause the second machine to malfunction.

Many machines are related and hate humans. This is called *Cybernetic Nepotism.*

Some machines belong to the same union. You can try negotiation. This is called *Cybernetic Arbitration.*

Some machines will work if you plead and beg enough. This is called *Cybernetic Foreplay.*

Most other machines have very intimate relationships and spread gossip about the operators. These are the most difficult machines. They are too busy with gossip to work. These machines are *Cybernetic Biddies.*

Psychological Behavior Required: Keep cool and say nice things to the machine. If you don't, it may spread rumors about you to the other machines. Nothing else seems to work! The most important factor is:

Never Let Any Machine Know You Are In A Hurry!

We hope the preceding helps. If you are having problems with any of your equipment, please take a coffee break. If the machine thinks you don't care, it may start working! If the problems persist, call us.

The following Note illustrates our capabilities and insight in recognizing and solving difficult systems situations.

Note #2: Trouble Shooting for More Experienced Personnel
(Older Guys)

On one of those rare days when everything was working properly, a sheet of paper requesting the installation of smoke detectors crossed my desk. As I read it, a realization of a *Basic Truth* came over me. So simple! So obvious we can't see it! I discovered what makes all electronic devices and circuits work.

Smoke is the thing that makes these devices work. Every time you let *smoke* out of an electrical or electronic device, it stops working! This can be verified through tests.

I was flabbergasted! Of course! Smoke makes *all* things electronic work. Remember the last time smoke escaped from your Lucas voltage regulator? Didn't it quit working? I sat down and grinned like an idiot as more of the truth dawned. I was obviously exhibiting strange behavior. The people in the office were starting to whisper and cast worried glances at me. My secretary took the rest of the day off. I must have looked like one of those people in a trance. You know, the kind you see in the science fiction movies.

It's the wiring harness that carries the smoke from one device to another in your MG or your Microcomputer. And when the harness springs a leak, it lets smoke out of everything at once and nothing works.

The starter motor on your car requires large quantities of smoke to operate properly. That is why the wire going to it is so big! The same logic applies to a computer printer.

Feeling very smug, I continued my hypothesis. Why are Lucas electronics more likely to leak than, say, BOSCH? Hmmmm. AHA!

Lucas is British! Things British always leak! British convertible tops leak water. British engines leak oil. British displacer units leak hydrostatic fluid, British "tyres" leak air and the British Government leaks defense secrets. So naturally, British electronics leak smoke!

There are very few problems with French products. French products seldom smoke. They usually don't work in the first place.

As for German products, they wouldn't dare fail!

Physical and Psychological Responses: Use smoke detectors to find problems with electronics. Using meters and analyzers is more frustrating, difficult and time consuming. Besides, by using these highly specialized electronic instruments, you may generate more smoke!

Another advantage is that smoke detectors do not require precise calibration. The use of electronic instruments for precise calibration of the smoke detectors is unnecessary.

We hope you find the above helpful in your organization. When we come up with more helpful hints, we will be sure to pass them on to you.

CHAPTER 28

DIAL 911

Many Independent Consultants operate as a cottage industry. The office in the home offers many benefits and some distractions. Most of my distractions are gone. The kids are grown and out of the house. The dog died. My wife works. I have a very quiet, peaceful, productive and uninterrupted environment.

Ah! The world of the home office. A FAX machine. An answering box. A personal computer. A modem. Business phone lines. Oh, well, I cheat a little and sometimes use my personal phone for the data communications connection using one of the modems.

One of my client's data communications phone prefix is 913. You can already see it coming. Right? Sure enough, in pressing the phone number via my keyboard, I hit *911xxxx*. Obviously the last four digits were ignored and I heard the emergency response from 911 through my modem. Now, the modem was not connected through a handset, so I could not talk back. I just disconnected.

Ah! Modern Technology.

The home phone rang. My wife answered it and heard the question. "Did you dial 911?" The 911 emergency number captures the source number calling. If there is a disconnect, they call back. My wife came into my office and asked me if I dialed 911. I said "yes" and asked (you never *tell* your wife anything) her to tell them I dialed it by mistake from my computer. She gave me one of her knowing looks and went back to the phone.

Now I am starting to get questions from my friends an associates, such as:

How does your computer know when to dial 911?

Does your computer dial 911 now when you threaten it?

Are there laws against computer abuse now?

There has been some kind of a security leak on my operations from my "home" office.

EPILOGUE

"It looks more like it does now than it did before I started."

John Benton
on completion
of this book.

Up to this point, most of my writing has been technical reports and articles that served as resource material for the book. My reasons for writing this book are mostly personal. It was a lot of fun, and I hope there is some useful information for those that have read it.

Many of the topics in this book could be expanded. If you wish, make comments or suggestions on what you would like to see in a future book. Please write to me at the publisher's address. Your comments about this book, especially *compliments,* will be gladly accepted, but *any response* will be appreciated.

A word of thanks is in order to those who helped with the book.

Jay Ohlrich did the cover and the sketches. Jay insisted that only his costs for the art work be paid and the rest given to charity.

Virginia McCullough did the editing and coordinating of typesetting and printing. Her encouragement and tolerance are greatly appreciated.

Bob Flynn, a long time friend and business associate, wrote the forward. He said he could handle the facts, but his wife Marilyn had to come up with nice things to say about me.

Most of all, my wife, June. She is very supportive, but is also wondering when I am going to stop writing and start making some money.

BIBLIOGRAPHY
& SUGGESTED READING

The Age of Discontinuity
Peter F.Drucker
Harper & Row

Critical Path
H. Buckminster Fuller
St. Martins Press

Entrepreneurial Telecommunications
Jim Jewett
ES Press

Friends in High Places
William L. Livingston
F.E.S. Limited Publishing

General Principles of Systems Design
Gerald M. & Daniela Weinberg
Dorset House Publishing

The Growth of Physical Science
Sir James Jeans
Cambridge University Press

Handbook of Walkthroughs, Inspections, and Technical Reviews
Daniel P. Freedman & Gerald M. Weinberg
Little, Brown & Co.

Have Fun At Work
William L. Livingston
F.E.S. Limited Publishing

How to Plan, Develop & Use Information Systems
Hein van Steenis
Dorset House Publishing

The Ideal Problem Solver
Bransford & Stein
W. H. Freeman and Co.

Megatrends
John Naisbitt
Warner Books

Nightingale-Conant
Insight Series and Tapes

The One Minute Methodology by E.Z. Systems
— as told by Ken Orr Dorset House Publishing

Peopleware, Productive Projects and Teams
Tom DeMarco & Timothy Lister
Dorset House

Rethinking Systems Analysis & Design
Gerald M. Weinberg
Dorset House Publishing

The Secrets of Consulting
Gerald M. Weinberg
Dorset House Publishing

Synectics
William J.J. Gordon
Harper & Row

The Tao of Physics
Fritjof Capra
Bantam Books

Understanding the Professional Programmer
Gerald M. Weinberg
Dorset House Publishing

ORDER BLANK

Telephone Orders: (708) 526-9321

Postal/UPS Orders:

Executive Information Development
121 South Drive, Tower Lakes
Barrington, IL 60010-1324

30 YEARS WITH COMPUTERS
(and other narrow opinions)

Number of Copies ______. **@ $19.95**

(6 or more copies - 5% discount,
free shipping if prepaid.)

SUBTOTAL (Books):	______.___
Shipping	$3.00
Additional (ea:)	$1.50
SUBTOTAL (Shipping)	______.___
Sales Tax: (Add 6.5% for books shipped to IL addresses)	______.___
TOTAL	______.___

Payment: ☐
Checks and Money Orders Only
NO CREDIT CARDS.

Please Bill: ☐
(Pre-Approved Credit Only)

SHIP TO:

Company Name ______________________________

Name ______________________________

Address ______________________________

City ______________________________

State _____ **Zip** ______________________________